LIVING IN THE PROMISED LAND

Living in the Promised Land

DONALD BRIDGE

KINGSWAY PUBLICATIONS

EASTBOURNE

Biblical quotations are from the
New International Version © International Bible Society
1973, 1978, 1984. Published by Hodder & Stoughton

Front cover photo: Sonia Halliday Photographs

British Library Cataloguing in Publication Data

Bridge, Donald
  Living in the Promised Land.
  1. Israel. Jerusalem. Social life.—
  Biographies
  I. Title
  956.94'4054'0924

  ISBN 0-86065-692-6

Printed in Great Britain for
KINGSWAY PUBLICATIONS LTD
Lottbridge Drove, Eastbourne, E Sussex BN23 6NT by
Richard Clay Ltd, Bungay, Suffolk NR35 1ED
Typeset by Nuprint Ltd, Harpenden, Herts AL5 4SE

Contents

My wife, Rita, was my companion in the adventures related in this book. She hardly appears in its pages because her wish has always been to take the quiet supporting role in my ministry. But without her there would scarcely be a ministry worth recording. To her I dedicate this book with affection and gratitude.

Acknowledgements

Lillian Morrison and Sheila Andrew worked patiently and skilfully at reducing my long-hand to a neat typescript. I salute them and thank them.

A number of organisations made my adventures and research possible. I am grateful to the Baptist Union of Great Britain and Ireland, Frinton Free Church in Essex, the British Friends of the Hebrew University, the department of Archaeology in the Hebrew University of Jerusalem, and Neot Kedumim (Garden of Israel). Various clergymen, professional guides and teachers taught me much. Sometimes I quote their names, sometimes I use pseudonyms, but to all of them (Jew, Gentile and Arab) I am grateful.

I must underline that my choice of material, my interpretation of the facts and my political and religious conclusions are solely mine, and should not be attributed to anyone else.

Foreword

The ancient land of Israel holds a compelling fascination for all who love the Bible. It has been the scene of so many important events in world history that give it a significance far beyond its physical size.

Donald Bridge combines his considerable skill as a writer with his knowledge of the Bible and his personal experience as chaplain of the Garden Tomb in Jerusalem. He gives a series of gripping descriptions of parts of the land of Israel that are associated with outstanding biblical events. These word-pictures bring the Bible alive and add new insights to aid understanding and spiritual perception.

Old Testament scenes from the history of Israel and New Testament references to the life, crucifixion and resurrection of Jesus all come alive in a new way for the reader, including those familiar with Israel.

Consideration is given in the final chapter to the biblical promises given to ancient Israel and their possible relevance to the modern State of Israel. Some readers may be surprised by the views expressed here, but even for those who take a different view, that will not detract from the value of this fascinating glimpse into the land of Israel and its vast spiritual heritage.

Once you start to read this book you won't be able to put it down!

Dr Clifford Hill

Part One

The Land

What is needed by the reader of the Bible
is some idea of the main outlines of Palestine—
its shape and disposition;
its plains, passes and mountains;
its rains, winds and temperatures;
its colours, lights and shades.
Students of the Bible desire to see a background
and to feel an atmosphere.

(George Adam Smith—Nineteenth Century)

The Lord your God is bringing you into a good land—
a land with streams and pools of water,
with springs flowing in the valleys and hills,
a land with wheat and barley,
    vines and fig-trees,
    pomegranets, olive oil and honey,
a land where bread will not be scarce
and you will lack nothing.

(Deuteronomy 8:7–9)

I

Where Prophets Walked

The plane banked and circled over the Mediterranean coast. Israeli music, joyous and spirited, echoed over the pilot's speaker-system. Sparkling turquoise sea, white hills and lucious greenery floated into view. The wheels bumped twice and now the plane was taxi-ing along the runway. The passengers applauded eagerly, as if surprised at our safe arrival. The volume of music increased. Several people were weeping. The speaker announced, 'Welcome to Israel.' Teenage girl soldiers with Uzi sub-machine guns waved us out of the aircraft and into buses. The air was palpable, ridiculously warm for 10 o'clock on an October evening, pressing on our faces, laden with the scent of oranges.

For Rita and me it was our sixth arrival in Israel, but this time we had come to live for an unpredictable period. Jerusalem would not now be a tourist wonder, but home.

The bus was winding its way through the Judaean hills already, as dusk thickened. Road-signs took us gasping into the world of the Bible. Jericho, 40 kilometers. Aialon, 2 kilometers. (The valley of Ajalon, of course, where the sun stood still at Joshua's command.) Bethshemesh over to the left—yes, where the men were gathering in the harvest when they looked up to see the plodding Philistine oxen bringing back the ark of the covenant. And where was it kept for a time? At Kiriath Jearim of course. We are passing it now, on a steep curve—Kiryat Iarim today. The names hardly change. This is where the Israeli food convoys fought their way up to relieve the starving city in 1948. Bombed and shelled from the steep hillsides, tyres flat and in ribbons, they jolted at 5 mph for an agonising four hours whilst yelling Arabs ran beside them firing at anyone who moved. Burned out shells of the vehicles lie by the road painted annually as a silent memorial to those who died in the attempt. Arabs died too.

Just over to the right again is the desolate ruin of Deir Yassim. It stands at the head of the valley where advancing Philistines were blocked by David's fledgling army. One night in 1948 a Jewish terrorist band massacred the villagers in order to frighten out of the area those who fed and hid the convoys' attackers. Another grim tale was added to the mythology of Middle East conflict.

Now Jerusalem was in view—perched on the heights, the walls and ramparts aglow in the spotlights. When our grandson first glimpsed it, he shouted, 'Look, there's heaven!'

Not heaven. Not by a long way. And yet mysteriously, mystically holy. So is the whole land. The Holy Land.

But what exactly do we mean by the Holy Land? Why does it exert such a fascination to hundreds of thousands of modern Christians? What can a piece of physical real estate say to us with any claim to be relevent to the gospel at the end of the twentieth century? In fact, its relevance is vital and twofold.

The Land fixes the gospel firmly in space and time.

There is nothing mythical about the Holy Land. The rocks are solid, the sand is gritty, the water is wet. Nazareth is not in fairyland; it is perched on the stony hills beside the Jezreel valley. Bethlehem is not a scene conjured up for Christmas cards; it is a town on the edge of the Judean hills. Jerusalem is not an ideal society to be built in England's green and pleasant land; it is 2000 feet above sea-level on the rising road eastwards from Tel Aviv. You cannot take a taxi or climb off a bus or go for a stroll in Israel without stopping at some physical spot and saying in wonder, 'God did this *here*...it happened *here*.'

This is vital. Not because the places carry some aura of holiness or grace, but because our faith depends on things that God said and did in particular places at a particular time. The gospel is *true*, in the simplest and most basic sense of that word. It is about things that really happened. Some religions depend on myth or symbolic stories which enshrine a mystical truth. Some religions major on cult, their virtue drawn from performing certain rites and ceremonies. But the Christian faith, and indeed the Jewish faith, is committed to fact. God is known by what he is seen to have done. The account of what God did, and his own explanation of why he did it are contained in the Bible. Drawing his certainty from those facts, the Christian says, 'the God who acted for my salvation in the life and death and resurrection of Jesus, can be known by me today. I surrender my will to him and put my trust in him.'

It is vital to say this in today's multi-culture of anything-goes subjectivism. 'Truth is true for you if it works for you—but of course something else works for me.' That is the existentialist argument of today's society, which permeates our literature, art, politics, morality and religion.

'Marriage made up of one man faithful to one woman for life is fine for you, if that's what turns you on. Just don't deny the validity of what turns *me* on, which is successive passing encounters consummated in different women's beds.'

'Jesus is your Saviour and friend? That's fine. I'm so glad

for you. As for me I get my kicks from soft drugs, and my friend is switched on to Buddha.'

This is today's atmosphere. In response to it, we need a message that says rather more than, 'You ask me how I know he lives? He lives within my heart.' That is certainly true, and I shall quote examples of its truth. Bishop Jenkins of Durham would be perfectly happy with that—whilst denying that Jesus ever came out of the tomb. But the Jesus who does indeed live in my heart is the Jesus who lives in objective reality whether or not I have welcomed him to my heart. He died on a physical cross for the world's salvation, whether or not any particular person believes it. He has opened the only way to God, whether or not some bishop has taken it. Before him every knee shall bow, whether or not the rulers of today's world believe it. The immense reality of Christ, his truth and his salvation in no way depend on our belief or experience: they are absolute and objective facts in their own right. *We* don't judge *them*: *they* judge *us*.

Living in the Holy Land constantly underlines the fact that our experience of Christ is based on solid historical fact.

Bethlehem. This is a real place. It perches on the long level line of hills that mark the old Patriarch's Way through Shechem, Shiloh, Bethel, Bethlehem, Hebron and Beersheba: names that cannot fail to strike us with their associations with Scripture.

Along this line the nomads of the middle bronze era drifted, their life-style now uncovered by archaeology in a hundred details that cast light on hitherto obscure and puzzling bible stories. Abraham's embarrassing scheme to father a baby on his wife's personal maid, Jacob's convoluted plots to grab the birthright, the terror of Joseph's brothers at the thought of losing their donkeys when they had no qualms about losing their honour...all of these stories reflect the reality of a way of life uniquely fixed in one passing era.

· But back to Bethlehem. Heart-broken, Jacob buried his wife Rachel there; the tomb still stands on the right of the Jerusalem-Bethlehem road as it enters the little town (Genesis 35:16–20). Israeli sentries lounge around it, ready to respond to Jewish-Arab rivalries. Ephathrah was its other name, but the source of its more familiar title can be clearly appreciated. 'Bet-Lechem' means 'place of bread.' The rich red soil washed down from the granite hills into Bethlehem's valley make it one of the very few places in Judea where barley can be grown. I've walked through the barley fields, deep green in startling contrast to the white sun-bleached slopes. Here, one of the world's great love stories relates, Ruth the Moabitess laboured to glean the sides of the fields as the destitute were allowed to do. Within a choice of only a few acres you can pinpoint the place. Boaz saw her, loved her—and the couple became ancestors of David and ultimately of Jesus.

Where the Philistines fled

Now we can see why young David was sent off to his brothers with food to supplement their army rations (1 Samuel 17). East of Bethlehem, the Elah valley begins to open up, ever widening until it breaks out into the coastal plain near Ashdod. Down there is Philistine country. Those frightening warriors, huge in stature, began to arrive on the coast as Israel appeared out of the desert. They grabbed the rich lowlands from Egypt's control and planted a city at the foot of each river; the famous five cities of Gath, Ashdod, Gaza, Ashkelon and Eglon.

They expanded by the obvious routes, sending raiding forays and eventually whole armies up into the heartland of Israel's hill country. Elah is the broadest and longest valley, thrusting within a few miles of Bethlehem. It was imperative for Saul's citizen-army to block the advance here. The point

.is underscored by the fact that Israel has a military camp there today, its great radar saucers pointing towards Philistine land, strung across the valley at the very point where David confronted Goliath. The monstrous man makes perfect sense in the story, incidentally. For these Philistines, known to archaeology as 'People of the Sea', were no less than survivors of the broken Mycanean Empire whose heroes' exploits were sung by Homer. What did *they* specialise in? The settlement of battles by personal one-to-one combat between champions, like Goliath. His great spear, by the way, was not *the size* of a weaver's beam (an absurdity) but *as* a weaver's beam—that is with a leather thong wrapped spirally round it causing it to spin as it was flung (1 Samuel 17:7). The first rifle bullet, in essence. An Israelite observer, with no idea of the principle behind it, would describe it in terms of something he understood.

There really is a stream bed, dry except in the brief winter, scattered with a profusion of 'smooth round stones' (1 Samuel 17:40). Rita and I took so many visiting friends to collect five each, that one day a jeep-load of Israeli soldiers were sent out from the nearby army camp to ask us what was going on. A little flustered, I began to explain about David and Goliath. As soon as I said, 'We are English,' they laughed heartily, shrugged and drove away.

All of these events can be related to known historical date, with a convenient date at the beginning of the Iron Age—say 1000 BC. In fact the Bible account refers to the immense advantage that Philistines had over Israelites: they knew how to smelt and work iron (1 Samuel 13:19).

Shepherds and Wise Men

The story leaps a thousand years. Bethlehem becomes the birthplace of Jesus—with immense significance, as an obscure and puzzling prophecy foretells (Micah 5:1–2, Matthew 2:3–6). The Place of Barley had by now become the centre for a guilt of carpenters and stonemasons. Its inhabitants' skills were passed on to their sons. Some emigrated to Galilee in the far north, but still looked to Bethlehem as their centre.

Rome instituted a new custom. The empire increasingly depended on the taxation of conquered countries. In 10 BC Caesar Augustus decreed a systematic census, beginning in Egypt and working northwards into Palestine and Syria. Subjects had to return to their town of origin for registration. It is the factual context for the story of Joseph's return to Bethlehem, his wife heavily pregnant (Luke 2:1–7). News of Jesus' birth was first announced to shepherds, of all people. But it makes perfect sense. Their sheep were, quite specifically in the *fields* (Luke 2:8–9). Sheep were not normally allowed in fields: their place was on the sparsely-grassed stony hills, not on the precious soil where barley could be grown *except* (said the Talmud) in the winter months between reaping and sowing. And even then, only if they were temple sheep reared for the sacrifices in the nearby temple (visible from the heights of Bethlehem).[1] These were no ordinary sheep and no ordinary shepherds. The announcement of the coming of the Lamb of God whose death would bring an end to the sacrificial system was peculiarly appropriate here. There was even a non-biblical tradition which pointed to 'the tower of the shepherds at Bethlehem' as the place at which Messiah would be revealed.

Two miles east of Bethlehem stands the sombre fortress of Herodium. King Herod's slaves built an extraordinary hidden fortress, like the inside of a volcanic crator, by shifting the top half of one hill to the summit of another. Herod the Great—otherwise known as Herod the Butcher —was a great politician, a brilliant architect—and a paranoic tyrant. Not born a Jew himself, and holding the throne (under Rome) by force and flattery, he feared above all else the attention of rivals. That fear drove him to murder his mother, one of his wives, and several of his sons. The naive question of the magi, 'Where is the one who has been born King of the Jews? We saw his star in the east' (Matthew 2:1–2) threw him into another frenzy of butchery.

Until recently there was no independent historical confirmation of the 'massacre of the innocents' in Bethlehem (Matthew 2:16–18). It was sufficient to say that the story exactly fits what we do know about Herod. The death of perhaps twenty baby boys would, in comparison to some of Herod's crimes, be too small to merit comment outside Bethlehem. Within a few months of that massacre we know that he had another son murdered, for exactly the same reason—he feared rivals to the throne.

Commenting on that killing, the Emperor Augustus drily remarked that it was safer to be Herod's pig than Herod's son (since Jews do not eat pork). Now a possible direct reference has come to light. The fourth century (pagan) writer Macrebius explains,

> When Augustus heard that Herod King of the Jews had ordered all the boys in Syria under the age of two years to be put to death and that the King's son was among those killed, he said "I'd rather be Herod's *hus* (pig) than Herod's *huios* (son)."

Joseph and Mary therefore fled with the infant Jesus to Egypt. It made sense, because Herod, once a close friend of Cleopatra's, had by now fallen out bitterly with her, and built Masada Fortress as part of a defensive network against her. Nowhere would a child suspected of threatening Herod's throne be more secure from extradition than in Cleopatra's Egypt!

Bethlehem, therefore, serves as a vibrant illustration of the historicity of Bible events, all of which are underlined by its geography, geology, botany and history. The Lamb sets the gospel firmly where God has put it—in the context of real life, real people, real places and real time. Real people still teach and live that gospel today…the Arab Christians of Bethlehem, some of them fine evangelicals.

There is a second comment to make.

The land illustrates and encapsulates truth about God and his people.

The very climate, topography and vegetation spell out a theology of One God, rich in mercy. This first dawned on me when I visited Neot Kedumim. This sprawling 500 acre patch of ground, the 'Garden of Israel', lies at the foot of the Ajalon valley. Its purpose is 'to show how the land of Israel became an inseperable part of the very essence of the Jewish people, and to explain the significance of this to…the Bible.'[2]

We bumped over rough tracks in a battered Land Rover. We tramped over stony hills, splashed across streams, scrambled through scented groves. We lay on our elbows scribbling notes and hunting up Bible references. Every shrub, flower, tree, grove and terrace held a message. Our Jewish guide, an agile and attractive middle-aged woman was a compendium of Scripture stories and talmudic lore.

It was more than a matter of mere references. Here, all around us, are the very soul and essence of the Word of God. I began to see the whole countryside as an extended parable. 'A land flowing with milk and honey,' our guide said suddenly. 'Do you know the reference?' She had soon picked me out as a Christian.

'Yes, of course. Moses' description of the promised land. Exodus and Deuteronomy.'

Her eyes twinkled. 'Right. Well, what does it *mean*?'

I hesitated. 'Well—a fruitful land, I suppose. A nice flowing symbol of fruitfulness.'

She laughed. 'Alright—but it is literal as well as symbolic. Where do you get milk from?'

'Cows,' I ventured hopefully.

She laughed again. 'Around here it's more likely to be goats. See them over there? Goats grazing on the highlands. Now what about honey? From bees, of course, who get it from the flowers in the lower meadows. So a land flowing with milk and honey is a land of goats and bees in the plentiful grasslands of mountain and meadow. Not like Egypt. Nothing like the wilderness.'

I knew she was teasing me. 'So what's your point? I'll buy it.'

'You're right: there's more to come. You see, when the Israelites arrived to occupy and settle the land, it ceased to be milk and honey. They ploughed up the meadows for grain and fruit. They terraced the mountain slopes for vineyards. See over here? Milk and honey means rich but uncultivated land. When God gave it to Israel, they changed it. Deuteronomy tells us again.' She turned to chapter 8 and read it aloud. I joined in from memory, which surprised and pleased her, and scored one point for me. 'The Lord your God is bringing you into a good land—a land with streams and pools of water, with springs flowing in the valleys and hills, a land with wheat and barley, vines and fig trees, pomegranetes, olive-oil and honey, a land where bread will not be scarce and you will lack nothing.' (Deut 8:7–9)

She snapped the Bible shut. 'Cultivated you see. Milk and honey is the land *waiting to be occupied* by us. Wheat and barley, vine and figs, fruit and olives and date-honey(not bee's honey this time)—that's agriculture in full swing. That's the land *in use* for us.'

She turned to me with a twinkle. 'Right, you know your Bible. Evangelical Christians do, I've noticed. Better than we Jews, as often as not. So you know about milk and honey in Exodus and Deuteronomy.... Anywhere else?'

I confessed that she had me stumped.

'Isaiah,' she said tersely. 'Isaiah 7 and verses 21–24, to get the whole sense. The prophet is threatening God's judgement on a forgetful and disobedient people. Look it up for yourself.'

A fairly masterful type, as Israeli woman often are: I meekly pulled my Bible out and checked it. 'In that day a man will keep alive a young cow and two goats. And because of the abundance of the milk they give he will have curds to eat. All who remain in the land will eat curds and honey' (Isaiah 7:21–22).

I looked up. 'You mean…?'

'Yes—judgement. The land invaded, the towns destroyed, the farms burned down, most of the population exiled. A few survivors left, living on what? Milk and honey. The sign of an empty land, lost again. See what verse 25 says: 'As for all the hills once cultivated by the hoe, you will no longer go there for fear of the briars and thorns'. You see? Back to the goats and the bees. So to Moses milk and honey meant a gift from God, ready to be gratefully used. But to Isaiah it meant the gift taken away again because his people didn't deserve it, weren't grateful for it, and couldn't keep it.'

Vastly intrigued, I did some research for myself. Winter evenings in east Jerusalem could be pretty dismal. Rain pattered against the windows, water gurgled down the sloping drainless streets, the minarets emitted their mournful moans, the radio only offered an occasional news-bulletin in English, and there was no television. But with a Bible, a concordance, a one-volume commentary and scribbled notes made after conversations with Jewish agriculturalists and Arab shepherds, I had material for fascinating exploration of ideas that made the dark evenings fly.

I went back to those fruits of the land listed by Moses, and recalled the first Sabbath dinner I attended at the University. 'Notice the Seven Fruits on the table,' a student had whispered. I checked rapidly. Loaves made of wheat and barley, wine produced from the vine, a bowl of mixed fruit with figs and pomegranetes to the fore, a jar of date-honey—but where was the olive oil? My friend nudged me and pointed to the Sabbath Candle, its double wick entwined. 'Candlewax partly made from olive oil,' he whispered. 'Stretching it a bit, I know; it used to be an oil-lamp of course. But the idea is there.'

The rabbi was intoning verses from the first chapter of Genesis as he broke the loaf open and poured wine gurgling out of the bottle into a cup. Gifts from God the creator to the world, but special gift of Jehovah to Israel. 'Be careful that you do not forget,' warned Moses.

I listed the Seven Fruits and began to research their characteristics. And made a remarkable discovery. As my charming guide at Neot Kedumim could have told me, balance is a very delicate thing in a land which straddles three continents and receives barely enough rain. The most crucial time in the agricultural year is the fifty day period between Passover and Pentecost, that is from mid-April to mid-June. During that period, the flowers of the grape, the pomegranate, the olive and the date all begin to open, and the little embroyonic figs begin to develop. At the same time, the kernels of the wheat and barley begin to fill out, developing from mere seed to become food.

It is a period when nature holds its breath. Everything depends on certain climatic conditions, but at that time alone, the climate is changeable. Winter sees guaranteed cold and rain (except in a disastrous drought). Summer is hot and dry and can never be anything else. But in Spring, hot *Khamsin* sand-winds from the south alternate with cold winds from north and west. The south wind is dry, the north or west breeze brings thunder, lightning, rain. Now, picture the situation. The swelling wheat needs moisture at first: later the rain would destroy it. If the needed rain lasts a few days too long it will damage the opening flowers of the grape, pomegranet, olive and date and prevent them pollinating. On the other hand, if the dry heat comes a few days too soon, the flowers will be happy but the wheat and barley will wither and fail to swell. One feels that it would need a computer to regulate it correctly! No—not a computer, but the Living God, providing for his people in his land. As the Neot Kedumim guide-book explained, 'The Bible underscores that only through a true understanding of the concept of the One Unifying God is it possible to comprehend the balance between the opposing forces which seem to determine the fate of the grain, wine and olive crops.'[3]

I began to see the picture. Here is a land where topography and climate, agriculture and economy, domestic life and eating habits all combine in a living parable that bears witness to One God. The great Jewish creed is the *Sh'ma Israel Adonai*—'Hear oh Israel, the Lord thy God is one Lord' (Deut 6:4). Their martyrs have died chanting it, their worshippers have prayed reciting it, their children have been nurtured repeating it. But the Lord says it too, in the very structure, vegetation and climate of the promised land.

Helmut Thielicke, a great preacher of the modern German church, analysing the technique of C H Spurgeon that even greater preacher to Victorian England, sees his secret as the gift of applying the Bible powerfully to the hearers' imagination and conscience.

> When Spurgeon speaks, it is as if the figures of the patriarchs and prophets and apostles were in the auditorium…. You hear the rush of the Jordan and the murmuring of the brook of Siloam, you see the cedars of Lebanon swaying in the wind, hear the clash and tumult of battle between Israel and the Philistines, sense the safety and security of Noah's ark, suffer the agonies of soul endured by Job and Jeremiah, hear the creak of oars as the disciples strain against the contrary winds, and feel the dread of the terrors of the apocalypse…. The heart is so full of scripture, that it leavens the consciousness, peoples the imagination with its images, and determines the landscape of the soul by its climate.[4]

Now what the Bible did in Spurgeon's hands through Spurgeon's God-anointed preaching, the Bible does in the hands of someone walking through modern Israel when the same Spirit is at work. Then the Land does indeed 'make the ubiquity of the Scriptures a real and living fact.' There is nothing automatic about it. But to the visitor whose senses are sharpened by faith, the whisper of God comes clearly.

It is this that makes Israel—Palestine truly 'the Holy Land'.

Notes

1.   *The Talmud*. Menahot 97a, Hagiga 27a.
2.   Nogah Hareuveni, *Nature in our Biblical Heritage*.
3.   Nogah Hareuveni, *Ibid* p 43.
4.   Helmut Thielicke, *Encounter with Spurgeon*, translated by John Deberstein (James Clarke & Co. Ltd., 1964), p 9.

2

Moonscape and Legends

Is there anywhere else quite like the Dead Sea basin? I doubt it. A great chasm in the earth cuts Israel off from its eastern neighbours and encloses the silent sinister sea that symbolises man's sin and God's judgement.

There it lies, as you come to the edge of the Judean desert. You can scramble downhill from ancient Arad, or take a taxi down the twisting road from Jerusalem to Jericho, made world-famous by the parable of the Good Samaritan. Sullen, oily and dull when seen close-to, the sea appears brilliant turquoise from a distance; an immense artificial swimming pool superimposed incongruously upon the grim, moonlike landscape.

Fifty-five miles long, ten wide, and a startling 1300 feet deep in places, it has another very great oddity. The shore and surface is over 1200 feet below sea level. Israeli guides will often enjoy their little joke as they bring their tourists down past the Inn of the Good Samaritan, and stop the bus at the first vantage-point of the plain below. 'Please slide your windows shut—we are about to drop below sea-level,' they say straight faced. Usually someone will do it— anxiously peering out to see if the water is seeping in!

Great limestone cliffs, seamed with fissures and riddled

with caves, fall in a curtain of rock, a thousand feet at a time, or in hundred-foot steps, to the barren shores of this strange stretch of water around which legend and Bible history, discovery and terror have gathered.

Here the grim judgement fell on vicious sensual cities of the middle bronze era known in and outside of the Bible as the Cities of the Plain. Abraham's nephew Lot escaped after receiving warnings from angels, but Lot's wife looked back and was engulfed. Next day Abraham gazed down from the Judean hills, 'and he saw dense smoke rising from the land, like smoke from a furnace' (Gen 19:28).

Nature and history, topography and chemistry, theology and scenery uniquely combine to illustrate and expound this awful drama of divine judgement on human wickedness. The very words sin, Sodom and Siddim conspire in onomatopoeic agreement. The empty precipices seem to symbolise desolation and forsakenness, suggestive of the very edges of hell, whilst the shimmering heat of the vast hollow, the desolate salt-pans, the grotesque rock formations and the lingering smell of sulphur all combine to turn long-past tales of judgement into daily warning that the wages of sin is death.

The Bible interprets the Genesis story both literally and symbolically. Clearly the overthrow of the Cities of the Plain is meant to be understood as a literal event. Airy attempts of liberal scholars and theologians to dismiss it as a typical legend, expressing subconscious race-characteristics fall flat on their faces, tripped over by the facts. Myths of fire from heaven and cities buried beneath the sea are indeed a common phenomenon. But in sober fact, the Bible never suggests for one moment that the doomed cities are below the sea in Atlantis-like ruin. Genesis describes burning sulphur raining from the skies, the cities 'overthrown' and the vegetation permanently destroyed, 'and smoke covering the land' (Gen 19:23–28).

Earlier incidents during the same generation suggest an

odd juxtaposition of fertile attractive land, populous towns, and a desolate and dangerous area full of tar-pits (13:10, 14:10 and 18:20). The land is clearly volcanic but something less than a volcano would be sufficient to match the description. Similar districts in America have seen cataclysms as a result of oil and gas pockets building up pressure until they burst through the rock and spurt burning oil into the sky, mingled with salt, sulphur and mud.

What happened to Lot's wife was not a kind of magic spell turning her into a pillar of salt in fairy-tale style (as children, and sometimes their teachers, often imagine). Lot was shamefully reluctant to leave the doomed city where he had settled in comfort and compromised his witness to God (19:18–20). His wife was even slower to take warning, and lingered short of the safety of the mountains, hanging back to sorrow over the loss of her sadly-compromised home. The convulsion overtook her, as they had been warned it might: 'Flee for your lives! Don't look back, and don't stop anywhere in the plain! Flee to the mountains or you will be swept away!'

Presumably she was caught and overwhelmed by the horrific burning mixture from the sky, which immediately cooled and hardened, so that where she stood there now stood 'a pillar of salt' (19:26). Guides today w'll obligingly point out solitary rocky pillars standing amidst the flat, featureless, sulphur-smelling salt-pans south-west of the sea: some of them bear an eerie resemblance to a figure hesitating and peering over its shoulder. Unfortunately, they would make the wretched woman between fifteen and twenty-five feet high!

Yes, it happened. The particular vices of the Cities of the Plain included 'wickedness and great sin against the Lord' (13:13); 'great and grievous sin' (18:20), and widespread sexual immorality, particularly of a homosexual kind (19:4–8). The very word sodomy has become in the English language (and until recently in English law) a synonym for this kind of vice.

The whole story of the overthrow of the cities offers a classic example of the principles that lie behind that most disliked and reviled truth that *God punishes sin*. The facts are all there. Sin is not merely against my neighbour but '*against God*' (13:13). The Almighty judge examines men's behaviour: 'I will go down and see' (18:21) carries the sense of arranging a trial and mustering the evidence. God is reluctant to punish and eager to forgive if there is penitence, and his verdict is always just: 'Will not the Judge of all the earth do right?' (18:25).

God's people have a role to play in intercessory prayer (note the remarkable dialogue between Abraham and God, 18:22–33). Where there is the slightest hope of a change of heart, God will delay judgement, send warnings and offer a way of escape (19:12–13).

However, not only is this incident literally true, but it holds symbolic significance. Its warning is reinforced and applied by Moses (Deut 29:23), by Amos, (4:11) by Isaiah (1:9) and by Jeremiah (23:14). Jesus turned the story inside out: the fate of the cities of Galilee to which he preached will be worse than that of Sodom and Gomorrah because these cities have seen and rejected more light, heard more truth and witnessed more evidence of the love and holiness of God (Matthew 10:14 and 11:20–24). New Testament writers Paul, Peter and Jude all refer to it (Roms 9:29, 2 Peter 2:6, Jude 7). The last book in the Bible takes up the theme again, and in stunning symbolism combines pictures of Pharaoh's Egypt, Lot's Sodom, the Jerusalem that crucified Christ, and the whole God-rejecting world-system as 'the great city, which is figuratively Sodom and Egypt, where also their Lord was crucified' (Revelation 11:8).

What the scientists say

Geologists give their own account of the Vale of Siddim. They tell us of a prehistoric sea that once stretched from Egypt to Syria, its surface broken only by the granite islands of Sinai's peaks. Huge deposits of limestone were laid upon this ancient seabed, so they say. Until one day (or century, or million years: geology can be prodigal with its years and vague in its speculations) the limestone rose under pressure from below and on each side, in long north-south folds. The result? The two parallel mountain ranges of Judaea, Samaria and Galilee on the west, and Saudi Arabia and Jordan-Syria to the east.

Not only did the mountains rise; the chasm between them sank. an immense fault developed, slashing down from snow-capped Hermon in Lebanon to the steaming waters of the Red Sea where it terminates in the Gulf of Akabah, 350 miles south.

Indeed, the great rift continues beyond that, for the Gulf itself is part of it, before it marches inland again, south-west across Africa until it reaches its awesome terminus in the Great Lakes of East and Central Africa.

Now the second fact comes into play. Not only is the great cleft garrisoned by mountain precipice; it is deep below sea-level. In sober fact, it is the lowest point on the surface of the earth. There is a deeper sea in Russia, but that lies at a higher altitude. There is a deeper valley in Antartica, but it lies under a mile of ice. There is a deeper rift below the Pacific Ocean, but the black waters lie above it. No—the Dead Sea holds the record, and has no rivals. Here alone you can stand on a silent shore and know that no man can stand any lower on this globe. 'Out of the depths I cry to you, O Lord' (Psalm 130:1). 'Where can I flee from your presence? If I make my bed in the depths, you are there' (Ps 139:7–8).

Of the whole area, with its frowning cliffs, its sullen sea

and its silent heat, it can be said truly, 'There may be
something on the surface of another planet to match it, but
on this earth there is nothing else like this deep, this colossal
ditch' (George Adam Smith).[1]

But a third physical fact has inter-reacted with the other
two to produce the unique, mysterious character of the
Dead Sea. The great sweep southwards of the deep rift is
broken and blocked before it leaves the Promised Land.

The two great parallel folds of mountain *connect*, forty-five
miles north of the Gulf. a diagonal ridge of limestone traps
the waters of the north and forms a funnel into a basin.

Fact and Fantasy

The result? Water runs into the Dead Sea but cannot run
out again. There it lies, steaming under the burning sun,
the effect heightened by sea haze that hang more densely
over this place than any other on earth. The waters running
in from the surrounding mountains carry the usual mineral
salts and more—for they run through nitrous soil and are
fed by sulphuric springs. The water evaporates in the intense
heat, forming a quivering translucent haze. The minerals
are left behind, in ever-increasing volume. The water of an
average ocean (bitter enough to our taste) contains 4–6%
solids in solution. In the Dead Sea it is an astonishing 32%.

A liquid that is one-third solid is going to have some odd
properties! No wonder strange stories abound throughout
history. The *Yam Hamelach*, the Salt Sea, was its ancient
name (Genesis 14:3). Aristotle told Alexander the Great
that no fish lived in its mysterious depths, and that a body
cast on its waters will float forever. When the Roman
Emperor Vespasian arrived with his conquering army he
heard strange tales of slaves who had escaped by running
across its waters whilst their frightened pursuers shrank
back. With the callous indifference to human suffering of a
tyrant, he ordered that anyone who could not swim should

be thrown in with their hands bound behind their backs. They floated. So may the modern visitor, if he wishes.

You can go home with the statutory snapshot of yourself reading a newspaper whilst lying on the water. You cannot actually swim because you float, your stomach about three inches below the surface, your back exposed, and your progress maintained by splashing and lurching along like a hippopotamus stranded on a submerged sandbank.

These bemusing characteristics have led to a stream of travellers' tales, superstitions and ridiculous exaggeration that mingle fact and fantasy. Clothes become instantly clean by immersing them in Dead Sea waters. Birds venturing to fly across its surface instantly drop dead. Its water holds marvellous medicinal powers, and is bottled and sold in Rome. Monsters lurk in its depths. It covers the mouth of hell. Jewish historian Josephus picturesquely described the sea 'coughing up black asphalt chunks that float on the water, looking like headless oxen.' The cursed cities of Sodom and Gomorrah lurked below the waters, still exercising a malign influence. So they say.

Early explorers

Consequently, until the nineteenth century the whole area was feared and shunned. Nothing factual was known about it. The first modern explorers only enhanced its mysterious and malign reputation. Ulrich Seelzen, a German adventurer arrived in 1806, having gone to the elaborate lengths of living in Syria for four years and converting to Islam, disguised himself first as an Arab and then a Greek Orthodox monk. He stuck to the eastern shore, mapped it carefully and discovered Herod's fortress of Machaerus where John the Baptist was beheaded. He could find no trace of the huge supplies of asphalt to which both Bible and travellers' tales bore witness (Genesis 14:10). They were awaiting discovery on the western side.

The first attempt to sail the waters combined elements of romance, eccentricity and tragedy. Christopher Costigan, a young Irishman, brought a small boat with him from Europe, met up with a Maltese sailor, mastered the art of sailing the craft on Galilee and the upper stretches of Jordan, then transported it overland to the Dead Sea. The frail craft zigzagged across the sullen sea, its tiny crew ill-equipped and scientifically naive. They took observations and measurements, bailed out the constantly-leaking boat and drank coffee made from the salt-laden water. It was August, with the heat at its most merciless, and Costigan went out of his mind, claiming to see the ruins of Gomorrah in the depths. The nameless Maltese sailor left the Irishman with Bedouins near Jericho and walked to Jerusalem for help. It came too late: Costigan died of fever, heat-exhaustion and dehydration.

There was, however, a curious sequel. A few months afterwards, John Stephens, American pioneer of Middle Eastern exploration, found Costigan's abandoned boat now constituting one wall of a hut in which he was sleeping at Jericho. He tracked down the Maltese, obtained the maps drawn on the ill-fated voyage, and published them. The mystical fantasy-sea was taking on clear shape. Almost immediately another German explorer, Von Schubert, hit on one of the scientific secrets behind the myths. Taking daily measurements of air temperature and barometric pressure, he suddenly began to find absurd readings which suggested that the sea was below sea-level! Clearly the instrument was broken. But as soon as he left the area, it seemed to mend itself. The truth dawned.

Along came the English. Lt Thomas Molyneux from *HMS Spartan* stationed at Haifa, transported a ship's boat to the area and sailed south from the exit of Jordan. Beset first by frightening storms, the waves striking the boat as if they were solid objects, and then by flat calms when the crew had to row and bail constantly in the gasping heat, they mapped out a wavering course but had to give up.

Molyneux survived the journey, but not for long. He had contracted malaria, was too exhausted to fight it, and died in Beirut.

It was high time that good old American know-how took a hand and tackled the thing professionally. In 1857 a complete expeditionary force from the US Navy brought three specially constructed boats (one appropriately named Uncle Sam under the command of Captain William Francis Lynch). They spent a month mapping, measuring, collecting specimens, drawing sketches, noting winds and currents and recording temperatures, weather conditions and atmospheric pressures.[2]

Science had arrived. The days of mystery were over, or so it seemed. But undreamed-of secrets were still to be unlocked.

Notes

1. George Adam Smith, *The Historical Geography of the Holy Land* (Hodder & Stoughton, First printed 1894), Chapter 22, pp 468–9.
2. For early explorations, see fascinating account in *Eretz* magazine Spring 1986, article 'Old Salts—Sailors, Scholars and the Dead Sea' pp 17–27.

3

Secrets of the Dead Sea

One torrid day in 1947 a Bedouin shepherd-boy, grazing his goats along the north-western shore of the Dead Sea, made a discovery which shook the archaeological world and brought the area into the newspaper headlines of a hundred countries. One of the goats scrambled into a cave part-way up a steep slope. The lad shouted, whistled, and lobbed a stone into the gloom. He heard a splintering noise. His missile had broken one of a row of large sealed clay pots hidden in the cave. The Dead Sea Scrolls were about to burst on an astonished world.

The pots (it eventually became clear) had stood there ever since some frightened scribe had hidden them from the grim advance of the Roman legions in their bid for a final solution to the problem of the Jews. No doubt he had hopes of retrieving them. It would have been beyond his power to imagine that they would stand there in the hot dry gloom for almost nineteen hundred years.

Hidden from the Romans, then rediscovered in a day of automobiles, aeroplanes, space-flight and nuclear fission— but what was in the jars? The contents proved to be a mini-library of ancient documents written painstakingly on animal skins sewn together and rolled into scrolls.

The story of how the scrolls eventually came into the hands of Israeli scholars is a drama in itself, comparable to 'King Solomon's Mines' or 'Raiders of the Lost Ark'. The area, at that time, was still part of the Kingdom of Jordan. The newly-created state of Israel was under attack from Jordan and ten other Arab nations, and fighting desperately for its life. A famous Israeli archeologist visited Arab Bethlehem on a public bus, bought three scrolls from a Greek antique-dealer, and smuggled them out under his shirt whilst snipers' bullets hummed past. Four other documents were illegally flown out of Jordan to America by a Christian priest who was determined to raise money from them for his war-stricken orphanage. Secret meetings with an Israeli cabinet minister led to their purchase for many times the price the monk had paid—and their surreptitious journey back across the Atlantic to Jerusalem. Others (including the fabulous Temple Scroll) took fifteen years to travel around the world and were tracked down via clues picked up in Moscow and in the Wall Street Journal. When, in 1967, the Israeli forces poured down the Mount of Olives and captured the ancient walled city of Jerusalem, a high-ranking minister was minutes behind the advance guard who stormed into the Rockefeller Museum outside Herod Gate. He courteously advised startled scholars still examining other scrolls that they now belonged to Israel, who would hold them in trust for the whole world of scholarship.

When, as a result of the same June war, the whole of the western shore of the Dead Sea was 'liberated' (as Israelis always smilingly put it), the army, the scholars and the politicians combined in scroll-hunting task-forces to hunt through thousands of caves. Little more from the First Century turned up, but another half-mythical page of Jewish history was uncovered by the discovery of letters and relics of the Bar Kokhba rebellion of 150 AD when the freedom-fighters actually reoccupied ruined Jerusalem for two years.

What did it all add up to?

One blazing April day I trudged across the sand-strewn rocks and scrambled up to the original cave where it all began. Looking down from it, I could see laid out before me the ruins of the Qumram Community of the Essenes, pin-pointed and excavated from the clues provided by the scrolls. For these mysterious documents have proved to be from the library of the Essenes—a group of Jewish religious enthusiasts not mentioned in the Bible, but described by Jewish and pagan writers in terms that had hitherto led to the assumption that they never really existed.

But they had existed. Stern, ascetic, passionately committed to the Law and the Prophets, led by a vaguely-sketched figure called the Teacher of Righteousness, they planted their monastic community in this wild and solitary place. And their library? It contained precious copies of whole sections of the Old Testament (older by a thousand years than anything that Jew or Christian so far possessed). There were commentaries on Bible passages too: fascinating insight into the way they read and interpreted the Scriptures. Their own Book of Discipline threw a flood of light on the principles and practices of the community. A strange book, 'The War of the Sons of Light Against the Sons of Darkness' bears some resemblances to the books of Daniel and Revelation. Here were fascinating books called Pseudographia—pious creations from the time between Old and New Testament, used by both Jews and early Christians, and including the book of Enoch, for example, which Jude 14 quotes but which was otherwise completely unknown to history.

Qumram and the Christians

I stood beside one of the five 'baptistries' in the ruins of the Community as one of Jerusalem's top scholars lectured. Later we examined the awesome Isaiah scroll, preserved in the Dome of the Scrolls opposite Israel's parliament in

Jerusalem—page after page sewn together vertically and occupying an entire curved wall.

What does it all really tell us about early Christianity?

At first there were the wildest rumours. Qumram was John the Baptist's headquarters. The feet of Jesus had walked these corridors. Jesus was brought up here as a child. The Teacher of Righteousness was either John the Baptist or Jesus. The apostles borrowed their teaching from the Essenes. The Bible was variously proved to be 'true' and 'untrue'. The whole of early Church history would have to be rewritten. And so on. Writers of fast selling and quickly forgotten religious speculations had a field-day.

Most of this was greatly exaggerated. The facts, simply, are these. The Jewish world of Jesus' time was rather more complicated than we had imagined. It was an era of great creativity and original thought, of excitement, expectation and fanaticism. The Essenes were dissatisfied with the Pharisees who interpreted the Law and the Sadducees who ran (and misruled) the Temple priesthood—and for pretty much the same reason as Jesus condemned those two groups. But the Essenes' reaction took them further away from Jesus not closer to him. In their extreme other-worldliness they regarded the narrow-minded Pharisees as careless libertines! What they would have thought of Jesus, with his emphasis on inner cleanliness not religious performance, defies the imagination!

We already know that Jews 'baptized' (plunged into water in a mikvah or ritual bath) Gentiles who were converted to their faith. They also had ritual purification for various situations (after childbirth, for example). Essenes took the thing further, and had ritual immersion for *themselves*, probably repeated every day.

The Essenes greatly encouraged the expectation of the coming Messiah (Christ), and saw themselves as fulfilling the vision of Isaiah 40:3. 'A voice of one calling: In the desert prepare the way for the Lord, in the wilderness make straight a highway for our God.'

Here there is an overlap with the New Testament story. It seems evident now that not only the Essenes lived in the wilderness of Judaea. Thousands of people influenced by them but not prepared to join them, went on short-term pilgrimages to camp in the wilds and prepare themselves for God's Kingdom. John the Baptist went to them—not calling crowds to come out there to hear him, but going there himself because that's where the crowds were—and no doubt attracting more by his presence: 'In those days John the Baptist came, preaching in the desert of Judaea and saying, 'Repent, for the Kingdom of heaven is near' (and Matthew then quotes the above Isaiah prophecy).

John's baptism, of course, was not a daily ritual cleansing but a once-for-all confession of sin leading to a change of heart and attitude—as his instructions made clear (Luke 3:7–14).

Speaking into the situation

Fascinating light, then, on the beginning of Jesus' ministry. He spoke into a situation ripe for his message. The wording of that message, too, has some bearing on Qumram. Readers of the New Testament have often commented on the striking difference between Jesus' reported 'style' as recorded in John's Gospel on the one hand, and Matthew, Mark and Luke on the other. Instead of simple workaday parables of the Kingdom there are strongly theological, technical, almost abstract themes.

Light and Darkness, Truth and Error, Life and Death: these are the subjects related by John. Why the difference? Scholars hostile to the truth and reliability of the Gospel accounts have often claimed an irreconcilable contradiction. 'This language of light and life and truth is not first century Jewish at all,' they have told us. 'This is the speech of second-century Greek thinking. John's Gospel has nothing

to do with John the fisherman or Jesus the Galilee rabbi.
Some second century Christian writer (perhaps in Ephesus)
has 'worked up' some of the Jesus miracle-stories and put
onto the lips of Jesus his own profound meditations on their
meaning.'

The scrolls give the dramatic lie to that. For some of them
are full of John's kind of language and they are firmly dated
as early first century Jewish writings from the vicinity of
Jerusalem. What presumably happened was that Jesus, the
master-communicator, adapted his language to the
thought-forms and themes current around Jerusalem (where
most of John's narrative is set). Just as, in Galilee, he used
the familiar scenes of Galilean life, in Samaria he took up a
woman on a subject that greatly excited the Samaritans,
and when facing the temple priests and teachers, argued in
their own idiom.

Of course what Jesus actually *taught* was totally different
from the doctrine of the Essenes. Far from being a development of their system, Christianity offered a drastic alternative.

I sometimes talked to a highly articulate bishop of an
ancient church, who lived on the Mount of Olives. The
'Church of the East' can trace an unbroken line back to the
early Christians of Galilee. Although its present membership is largely Arab, its character is extremely Jewish. They
observe the Passover, for example, and their liturgical
language is a development of the Aramaic which Jesus
presumably spoke.

The bishop assured me that disillusioned survivors of the
disbanded Essenes were converted to Christianity after the
destruction of Jerusalem (at the time when the scrolls were
hidden). The failure of their expectations must have been
painful. Rigid law-keeping (and more than the law required)
had *not* brought the Messiah. The Children of Light had *not*
overcome the Children of Darkness (the Romans) in war—
just the opposite. How ripe they must have been for a

Messiah who changes the inward nature, a kingdom that is not of this world, a conquest of sin and death won by one who died on a Roman cross, a baptism that spoke not of ritual requirements but of the passage from spiritual death to new life!

The romance of the copper scroll

One of the most extraordinary scrolls lies at the heart of a drama still being played out today, which bears all the marks of a Rider Haggard romance.

Vendyl Jones is a unique character. Scholar, explorer, adventurer, theologian, treasure-hunter, he is an American Baptist who has wholly embraced Judaism. Indiana Jones, the lead character in the tongue-in-cheek adventure film 'Raiders of the Lost Ark' is said to be drawn from Vendyl Jones, with suitable embellishments. I have a photograph of him standing under the searing Dead Sea sun, engrossed in conversation with Israel's Chief Rabbi and a leading politician. They are standing outside yet another Dead Sea cave. The subject of their talk is the search for the ashes of the red heifer, one of the most mind-boggling quests of Jews and Christians together, which brings to one focus the methods of modern science, the aspirations of Israel in the 1980's, the enthusiasm of American Evangelicalism, the fate of Jewish freedom-fighters at the hands of the Romans nineteen hundred years ago, and the instructions of Moses in another desert fifteen hundred years before that.

It has its origin in the instructions Moses gave for the 'purification' of instruments used in worship, and for the priests involved in sacrifice. A young cow was to be killed and burned entire with wood, hysop and scarlet cloth. Then, 'Gather up the ashes of the heifer and put them in a ceremonially clean place outside the camp. They shall be kept by the Israelite community for use in the water of cleansing; it is for purification of sin' (Num 19:9).

David, in his penitence after the affair with Bathsheba, prayed 'Cleanse me with hyssop and I shall be clean; wash me and I shall be whiter than snow' (Ps 51:7). He would be thinking of this ceremony, and its inner significance.

In Jesus' day (the rabbinical writings tell us) the animal was burned on the slope of the Mount of Olives, directly opposite the Eastern Gate through which the Altar of Burnt Offering could be seen in the Temple, and the Holy of Holies high behind it (curiously enough, the spot must have been very close to the Garden of Gethsemane). One third of the ashes, we are told, was kept in the Temple, one third reserved on the Mount of Olives, and one third dispersed and hidden amongst the priests. Necessarily so for there had to be continuity: 'This will be a lasting ordinance' (Num 19:10).

Now since the temple and all its contents were destroyed in AD 70, the sacrificial system cannot be restarted. There is no way to purify the priests and their instruments except by employing the last ashes used a generation after the time of Jesus! Thus the hopes of some Jews and some Christians of a restored temple are impractical (we shall return to this topic of a Third Temple).

Unless of course in those final dreadful days when Jerusalem was put to the flames...just suppose that someone hid the ashes of the red heifer, with a view to one day restoring temple worship?

Well—the crazy idea is not so crazy after all. One of the Dead Sea Scrolls, lying unread for years since its discovery, has yielded another stunning secret. It is made of thin copper plates rolled together, and, after undisturbed centuries, oxidised and hopelessly fused together—until English technology and ingenuity was focused on the problem. Dr H Wright Baker of Manchester College of Science and Technology coated the whole black, green and bronze mess with plastic to prevent shattering, and then patiently sliced through the fused layers with a tiny saw used to slit pen nibs. The separated pieces were then reconstructed in order, and the mysterious message was ready to decipher. It proved dramatic enough: an account of how priests hid temple furniture and treasure during the last terrible days of that Roman War. In the style of every good thriller, some of the message is in code. But one thing was clear. The treasure which the priests had hidden had included a pot containing the last-used ashes of the heifer! The hunt for the ashes was on!

It was the moment for Vendyl Jones to step in. An expedition was launched by this extraordinary character who as we have said, began as an American Southern Baptist pastor, studied Hebrew religion and language from childhood-standard to university and beyond, and embraced an extraordinary version of Judaism which maintains that Jesus is the Jewish Messiah and the Gentile Saviour, but that the Jews don't need a Saviour because they are already Jews. Having correctly predicted the 1967 Six Day War from Jesus' Olivet Discourse in Matthew 24 and scored again by finding the name of the next Chief Rabbi from the same source, he fought in the Israeli Defence Forces, helped to develop a new bank, and took on the training of Christian Guides for the Israeli Government.

One of his assistants telephoned me when I appeared on the prestigious Marlon Maddox radio chat-show in Dallas, Texas. The guest at this event has the opportunity to speak on a favourite subject and answer phoned-in questions for ninety minutes (the audience touches ten million). My subject was Israel and the Christian. An excited archaeologist asked a question about the significance of the ashes of the red heifer. I was able to give a Christ-oriented answer (to the surprise and amusement of my radio host). Afterwards the questioner rang again and told me at length about the expedition being mounted. The probable cave had been identified. Excavations had been started. The Chief Rabbi had ten boys ready under Bar Mitzvah age (and therefore ritually not sinners, since they had not yet embraced the Law), and their task would be to carry the ashes in triumph from the Dead Sea area to Jerusalem. Israeli citizenship was being offered to any Gentile who gave financial or physical help to the excavations.

My informer expected me to be as excited as he was. From the archaeological viewpoint, of course, I was. Such a find, if it is made, would rate with the very greatest of all time. Theologically, and speaking as a committed Christian, I find myself less enthusiastic. After all I need no sacrificial system. Its restoration (in Jerusalem or anywhere else) would add nothing to that wondrous sense of pardon and access to God that is the heritage of every believer in Jesus, of whatever race. The anonymous writer to the Hebrews says it all in the New Testament.

> The blood of goats and bulls and *the ashes of a heifer* sprinkled on those who are ceremonially unclean sanctify them so that they are outwardly clean. *How much more*, then, will the blood of Christ...cleanse our consciences from acts that lead to death, so that we may serve the living God! (Heb 9:13–14)
>
> Day after day every priest stands and performs his religious duties; again and again he offers the same sacrifices, *which can never take away sins*. But when this priest (Jesus) had offered for all time one sacrifice for sins, he sat down at the right hand of God...because by one sacrifice he has made perfect forever those who are being made holy. (Heb 10:11–14)

Viewed, then, as a means of salvation and an opening of the way to God, the search for the famous ashes could be seen as an irrelevence—even as a red herring across the path. But viewed as a Jewish exercise in rediscovering their roots, it can be watched with great sympathy by the Christian observer. The last I heard, the 'Cave of the Column' had yielded some clues and supplied some obstacles. Apparently at the entrance to a further branch-tunnel some way inside, an elaborate arrangement of rocks not only blocks further progress but acts as a kind of booby-trap. This makes eventual discovery of something fascinating all the more likely. Meanwhile, Chief Rabbi Solomon Gonen says to Christian and Jewish volunteer workers from America, 'You are working for the good of the Jewish people around the world. You do all this and ask for nothing in return for yourselves. I tell you that you have already found a treasure! You are the treasure!'[1]

The excavations have continued from 1983 until 1988 as I write this. Slow work. But the Dead Sea requires a lot of patience.

Notes

1. Rabbi Gonen quoted on cover of *Will the Real Jesus Please Stand?*, Vendyl Jones (Priority Publishers USA), 1983.

4

Promise of New Life

We bumped the car over a section of the road broken up by recent flash-floods. Two days ago, for a couple of hours, rushing water four feet deep and fifty yards wide had carried the contents of a brief thunder-shower over the Judean desert, cascading down fissures in the thousand-feet curtain of rock, across the reed-grown saltplains and into the bitter embrace of the Dead Sea. Friends of mine had been trapped on the wrong side whilst hiking—and had watched a tourist bus helpfully nose its way across, pushing in front of it a small car whose terrified occupants had become marooned halfway.

Now the ground was not even damp. Lizards scuttled across dry stones, and a harmless snake wound its lazy way over the baked sand. We were looking for Nachal David (David's Spring) near that startling oasis of life and greenery called En Gedi from David's day until now. The Bible tells how the future King fled here from Saul's paranoic jealousy. His choice of a hiding-place had plenty of precedent already, and has been emulated often enough since. 'The strongholds of En Gedi' (1 Sam 23:29) are cave-riddled cliffs like so many others in this dry silent place, but with one difference. The perennial spring still runs when flash-floods are only a

dim memory of early spring. 'The Crags of the Wild Goats'
(1 Sam 24:2) still bear that name 'crags' for obvious reasons,
and 'wild goats' are attracted by the guaranteed water
supply.

We scrambled along the stream-bed, sometimes sandalled
feet in the water sometimes stone-hopping, and occasionally
feeling our way along the crumbling bank.

We were in an eerie green tunnel formed by the huge
rushes which grow in profusion on each side and bent above
to form a roof. In constant gentle movement, they whispered
and rustled as if sharing with each other the secrets of the
Dead Sea.

Now the path zig-zagged across the crags, and we were
out in the open, feeling that splendid dry heat that warmed
my back through my shirt and warmed the orange-squash
in my two water-bottles so that my statutory pint-an-hour
drink was actually hot.

We stopped, nonplussed at a wooden notice which warned
us that leopards have returned to this area. We should be
very careful about this, it seems, for leopards are protected
animals. Apparently, upon meeting a member of this saga-
cious species, one should look it firmly in the eye, and back
away quietly. But no sudden movements please, as these
disturb leopards. I reflected on how difficult it would be *not*
to make a sudden movement if confronted by a leopard!
And what is an *un*disturbed leopard like, I wondered?
There are further helpful hints. Don't throw stones at it. It
would be best if there are at least five of you in the party.
(What do the other four do? Gang up on the leopard and
chase it away, without disturbing it of course?) Two
remaining instructions are heavily underlined. 'If you are
attacked by a leopard, be sure to report the fact to a
gamewarden' (why? so that he can render you first aid? or
check whether the leopard found the experience disturbing?). And 'Always remember that leopards are protected'
(protected from *what*? What about *people* being protected?). I

have never decided whether this notice is to be taken seriously, or whether it is a subtle example of Israeli humour!

At any rate, we met no leopards that day, and the climb (as now it became) was uneventful but rewarding. It was easy to see how Saul could employ a search-party of 'three thousand chosen men' and still fail to locate David. The story, and its famous sequel, is told in 1 Samuel 24. The sheepcotes mentioned there are still visible: little walls of loose stones around the mouths of the more accessible caves. The sheep can retreat into the cool interior when the sun is unbearable. That may be why Saul never heard David's stealthy approach amidst the shuffling of sheep and goats. W M Thompson, writer of that old classic *The Land and the Book*, describes seeing sheep actually tramp past a sleeping herdsman in such a cave entrance, without waking him.

It is also noticeable that when we looked into the cave from outside, as Saul would have done, the darkness seems impenetrable, whereas looking towards the opening from inside, as David would, everything is visible.

In fact Saul was not actually asleep this time. That was on a similar occasion a few miles away. This time he was tactfully using the cave as a toilet, and the Authorised Version employs similar tact in obscuring that fact (as it does in the later story of Elijah and the priests of Baal [1 Kings 18:27]. There the prophet, jeering at the priests for their god's non-intervention, ribaldly suggests that he may be spending a long time in the toilet. These prophets could display an earthy sense of humour!). This makes the circumstances of David's removal of a small piece of clothing all the more humiliating for Saul, and afterwards the magnanimous fugitive was conscious-stricken (1 Sam 24:5).

The scene shortly afterwards could be readily imagined as we stood there. David could stand easily within sight and sound of Saul to display his little trophy and declare his peaceful intentions, yet so high up the precipitous side of

the ravine to make pursuit impossible. It would have taken
the King's men an hour to reach the spot. We tried it and
lost our nerve under a wilderness of rocks, more caves,
ravines, and shimmering heat that confuses the senses. 'And
Saul wept aloud. "You are more righteous than I", he said.
"You have treated me well, but I have treated you badly...
May the Lord reward you well for the way you treated me
today. I know that you will surely be King"' (vv 17,19).

A place of refuge

David was not the last to make this lovely ravine a place of
refuge. Excavations by Binyamin Mazor in 1962 showed it
to have been a flourishing centre of life, religion and com-
merce during that last great crisis through which Jeremiah
lived. When Nebuchadnezzar took Jerusalem by storm, a
hoard of silver ingots was hidden here, and has been
unearthed. After the return from exile (under Ezra and
Nehemiah) the place prospered again. Several articles from
that time bear the word *yehud*, which is Persian for Judah.
Could these have been some of the supplies carried by
Ezra's expedition which was equipped in Persia? 'All their
neighbours assisted them with articles of silver and gold...
and with valuable gifts' (Ezra 1:5-6).

Imagine the emotions of those who packed their goods
and labelled them for far-off Jerusalem! It was a half-legen-
dary city from which God had banished their grandparents
in holy anger. Now his promises of grace and forgiveness,
uttered by the prophets even as they warned of doom, were
to be fulfilled in them!

The place again became a centre for the production of
perfume, and Professor Mazor discovered the restored vats,
already ancient at the time of Solomon.

Solomon's love song refers to them. 'My perfume spread
its fragrance...from the vineyards of En Gedi' (Song 1:12-
14). Two hundred years later, En Gedi was once again a

place of refuge. A citadel has been unearthed, built there in the third century BC when the Maccabees were struggling desperately to defend home and religion against the vicious Greek attempt to assimilate them or crush them. History leaps forward again, and the crags of the goats are found hiding the Zealots—urban guerilla freedom-fighters who still held out when the Romans had sacked Jerusalem, in fulfillment of Jesus' solemn warnings. And then again, evidence points to En Gedi as one of the bases for the Bar Kokhba Rebellion of 150 AD which for one brief heady span reoccupied Jerusalem and set up an independent Israel.

The Zealot's Last Stand

We returned safely to the Dead Sea shore (no leopards) and continued on to the most spectacular of all the refuge places. The massive bulk of Masada, a rock thirteen hundred feet high with its queer boat-shaped plateau, stands as a memorial to Israel's last defiance of Rome. Here the grim drama of the Jews' hopeless struggle against the superpower was played out to its glorious, heroic, pointless climax.

Herod the Great had built a fortress-cum-palace here when he fell out with Cleopatra of Egypt. (Yes, *that* Cleopatra!) Josephus, a generation after Jesus, described its lavish appointments, in terms that have been regarded as exaggerated for centuries, but now prove to be accurate. Bath-houses, gardens, government house, hanging palace, vast storage-barns, immense water-cisterns—all have now been found.

When Herod was long-dead, and the Romans had captured Jerusalem, remnants of the Zealot movement took refuge in the mountain fortress, having taken the Roman garrison by surprise. With one winding path wide enough for just one man at a time, and cisterns that collected the few weeks' rain in such quantities that it could supply them for years, the rebels were in an almost impregnable position. Over nine hundred of them (including wives and children) not only made it their home but ventured out on guerilla forays.

Eleazar ben Yair, a Galilean, was the leader, with a flair for improvisation, underground warfare, administration, and tub-thumping eloquence. General de Silva of the Tenth Legion was given the thankless task of reducing the fortress. His troops had to bring every drop of water from En Gedi, 10 miles away, and every other provision from Judea, 35 miles away. They had no shelter from the merciless sun.

Silva set to with the usual Roman thoroughness and patient discipline. A stone wall was built around the entire mountain, to keep the rebels inside. At least six large military camps were erected: the soldiers were here to stay, until the job was done. You can scramble along the remains of the wall, and squat in the ruined officers' quarters of the camps.

Then they really got down to business. Silva's military engineers began to build another hill, an immense sloping ramp of rocks and earth leaning against the northern side of the mountain. Up this, in due course, a huge wheeled tower and battering ram would be pushed and pulled by hundreds of sweating men on ropes and pulleys.

At first the Jewish defenders killed the builders with showers of rocks, arrows, spears and boiling oil. The Romans then brought in Jewish slaves captured in the recent war—and the missiles stopped.

After eighteen months the ramp was complete, the mobile tower in place, and the defenders doomed. The night before the final assault, with the gate already in flames and the fortress walls breached, the Zealots held their last conference. Eleazar made his final speech

Let us at once choose death bravely; let us have pity on ourselves, our wives and children. For we were born to die, we and those we have brought into the world…. But outrage, slavery, and the sight of our wives led away to shame with our children — these are no necessary evils…. Come, while our hands are free to hold the sword, let them do a noble service. Let us die before we become slaves, and leave this life together as free men with our children and wives!… Let us therefore make haste, and before affording (our enemies) their hoped-for pleasure at seizing us, leave them to be dumbfounded by our death and awed by our fortitude.[1]

The men acted immediately. Each went to his home, and under pretext of embracing wife and children, killed them by swiftly cutting their throats. Then setting fire to the storehouses (still heaped with enough food for several years seige) they drew lots to choose the ten who would kill the rest of them.

Then each laid himself down beside his wife and children, and flinging his arms around them, exposed his throat to those who had to perform the painful office…so finally nine (of the ten) bared their throats, and he who was last of all, set the palace ablaze, and then, summoning all his strength, drove his sword right through his body and fell dead beside his family.[2]

When the triumphant Romans smashed through the gateway next morning, they found silence and death, and a victory turned to ashes. Two women and three children had in fact hidden and survived. They related the grim tale.

Pop-star archaeologist

In 1965 that colourful figure Yigael Yadin led a great combined effort to unlock the secrets of Masada. Even its location was not entirely certain although the claims of several scholars and explorers did in fact prove to be correct. Hundreds of Jewish and non-Jewish young people gathered from America and Europe to assist in a unique 'dig' to discover remains, not underground, but on top of towering rocks (albeit covered with shapeless rubble and drifted sand).

It was a dramatic success. Detail after detail of Josephus' description were uncovered! The 'hanging palace', for example, is built on three natural steps down from the edge of the twenty acre plateau, hanging at a dizzy height over the dramatic landscape, and frightening even now when it is provided with metal rails and stairs. The half-burnt corn was still in the vast storehouses. With his well-known flair for the dramatic, Yadin recorded and published every incident. In the palace ruins 'a thick layer of ashes, the product of a powerful fire...were coins struck during the revolt, with such typical inscriptions as 'The freedom of Zion'...it was clear that we were bringing to light the remains of that very fire mentioned by Josephus.'[3]

Even more astonishing, the probable lots cast by the grim ten were discovered: '...eleven inscribed pieces of pottery, and upon each was a single name, each different from its fellow.... Had we indeed found the very ostraca which had been used in the casting of lots? The probability is strengthened by the one bearing the name Ben Yair, which could have referred to no other than Eleazar Ben Yair.'[4]

The outline of the inexorable ramp is easy to distinguish from the natural cliffs. A synagogue gives evidence not only of the more pious amongst the rebels, but of the fleeing of some of the Qumram Community to this false refuge. A few scrolls (or fragments of them) were found—snatches from Ecclesiastes, Leviticus, Psalms, and a non-biblical book called Songs of Sabbath Sacrifices. But most startling, almost unbelievable in its unique appropriateness, was a well-preserved section of the Prophecy of Ezekiel, hidden under the synagogue floor. It is Chapter 37, the famous Vision of the Valley of Dry Bones. Here is the most picturesque promise of Israel's national and spiritual restoration surely ever penned. The eerie valley was piled with bones,

'bones that were *very* dry.' Then a strange question was addressed by God to the prophet, 'Can these bones live?' (Ez 37:2–3).

The prophet's faltering reply was summed up by an American preacher: '"Can these bones live?" The prophet looked at the bones and he daren't say "yes". He looked at the Lord and he daren't say "no". So he passed the buck, and said "Lord thou knowest".'

Then comes the play on words, with the Hebrew *ruach* meaning 'wind', 'breath', 'spirit' (human) or 'spirit' (divine). The prophet speaks to the bones, the bones come rattling together to make complete skeletons, flesh covers them—then the Wind blows and 'breath entered them; they came to life and stood up on their feet—a vast army' (37:10).

From cemetery to parade-ground! No wonder the archaeologists were awed by the appropriateness of the Scripture for the time it was buried, and for the time it was rediscovered. 'I will put my Spirit in you and you will live, and I will settle you in your own land. Then you will know that I the Lord have spoken, and I have done it' (37:14).

The vision was given and recorded around 600 BC, as the Babylonian world-power crushed Jerusalem and sent men like Ezekiel and Daniel into lifelong exile. Its first fulfilment was less than a century later, when some Jews returned from what was by then the Persian Empire. There was indeed a new spirit within them, never again would they drift into that idolatry which had dogged their history so far.

But when that particular scroll was copied from a copy of a copy of a copy, Jerusalem was once again under the Gentile heel and a long bitter exile was beginning which the scribe who hid it could never have imagined in his wildest moments of pessimism and despair. Nineteen centuries! Until, in the mid-twentieth century, Israel became a home once more for Jews from a hundred lands which that scribe had never heard of. Then they dug. And the scroll he had secreted came to light, as its promise was fulfilled.

Whatever the political, economic and military rights and wrongs of the Middle East crisis (and none of it is as simple as some Israelis and some Christians believe), one cannot but see God in these events, working out purposes more wise and all-embracing than any of our prophetic schemes.

Promise of renewal

And, of course, the great promise of this dramatic chapter has wider implications. Ezekiel is, above all others, the Prophet of Renewal. In vivid metaphor and symbol (of wind and spirit and throne and river) he repeatedly tells us that *God is the God of new beginnings*. He can take the most despairing situations of God's people, whether Israelite or Christian, and bring the breath of renewal and restoration. Jesus in his night interview with Nicodemus, expressed surprise and reproach at that religious leader's inability to understand the need to be 'born of water and of the Spirit.'

He was saying in effect 'Come on Nicodemus! Water and Spirit! Remember Ezekiel 36 and 37!' The sprinkling with clean water, the new heart and new spirit. The Wind that blows and brings an army of skeletons to life; this is the Father's *promise* (John 3:1–15).

A recurring cycle of declension, apostasy, and judgement followed by repentance, forgiveness, restoration and renewal. That seems to be the warning of Scripture and the promise of God's grace. It is also, clearly, the actual history of the people of God. The Reformation and the eighteenth century Awakening are the two best-known examples to western Christians. Russian Christianity before and after the Revolution furnishes an example further east. Has it happened in China, in our own time? To South America? Is it happening in the modern Renewal movements? Certainly whenever believers have looked for it and longed for it, revival has appealed to their prayerful imagination in this picturesque language of Ezekiel 37 and the Valley of Dry Bones.

Take a page from John Wesley's 18th Century diary.

> 1765. I met a man called William Rowe. He told me— "I was going over Gulval Downs and I saw a crowd of people together. I asked what was the matter and they told me a man was going to preach. I said, it must be some lunatic. But when I saw you, John Wesley, I said This is no lunatic. You preached on God raising the dry bones, and from that time I could never rest till God was pleased to breathe on me and raise my dead soul."

Ezekiel brought together total commitment to God's already revealed Word (in Law and Psalm and Prophet) and a burning vision of the now-activity of the Spirit of God. Times of Revival always see that combination. Not Word alone, merely the grim holding on to the old truth and the complacent assertion that we, at any rate, hold to it when others abandon it. Not Spirit alone which, unchecked and untested by Word, may not be *Spirit* at all, but merely human excitement and enthusiasm. But Word and Spirit together. As one of Britain's finest biblical preachers today says, 'We need a spirituality of Word *and* Spirit, as in Ezekiel's valley of dry bones. We need an unashamed commitment to the Bible as the supreme and primary source of our knowledge of God, *but also* an openness to the contemporary leading of the Holy Spirit in the hearts and minds of Christian men and women' (Roy Clements).[5]

We drove back from Masada to En Gedi. Ezekiel's scroll had stirred another memory, and I wanted to check on it. The same prophet has another marvellous picture of Holy Spirit Renewal.

> I saw water coming out from under the threshold of the temple towards the east.... He led me through water that was ankle-deep...knee-deep...up to the waist...but now it was a river

that I could not cross, deep enough to swim in.

Then he led me to the bank of the river…I saw a great number of trees on each side. He said to me, this water flows down into the Arabah, where it enters the Dead Sea. When it enters the Dead Sea, the water there becomes fresh. Swarms of living creatures will live wherever the river flows…. Fishermen will stand along the shore; from En Gedi to En Eglaim there will be places for spreading nets (Ezekiel 47:1–10).

Fishing at En Gedi! This is a modern Israeli saying, whether consciously related to Ezekiel I cannot ascertain. No one I've heard quoting it was aware of any biblical reference. It is an Israeli figure of speech for 'trying the impossible'. For, of course, there are no fish at En Gedi; it stands by the Dead Sea, where nothing lives. 'I've been fishing at En Gedi', an Israeli will say, humorously, when he admits to tackling the impossible—like arguing with the income tax inspector, or making ends meet during 400% inflation, or persuading his wife to change her mind. They try to fool ignorant tourists with it, too—and often succeed. 'Be sure and do some fishing at En Gedi' they will gravely advise naive visitors.

But when the Spirit of God moves, the impossible becomes possible. The stream of life and healing flows from the Throne of God. The impossible is done. They catch fish at En Gedi. We stopped, and pondered, and prayed at the place of perfume. Then on we drove, until the Jerusalem road snaked upward and the place of death and judgement was behind us. And—yes—G K Chesterton was right when he came here in 1918 and claimed there was a spot where you could look down and see the place of Sodom, and up to catch a glimpse of the church tower on the place of Ascension at Olivet.

Below me all the empire of evil was splashed and scattered upon the plain, like a wine-cup shattered into a star. Sodom lay like Satan, flat upon the floor of the world. And far away and aloft, faint with height and distance, small but still visible, stood up the spire of the Ascension like the sword of the Archangel lifted in salute after a stroke.[6]

Notes

1. Josephus, *The Jewish War*, Bk VII para 380–388 pp 498–499.
2. Josephus, *ibid* Bk VII para 395–397 p 500.
3. Yigael Yadim, *Masada* p 54.
4. Yigael Yadim, *ibid* p 197.
5. Roy Clements, 'Word and Spirit', *The Bible and the Gift of Prophecy Today* (UCCF Booklet 1987).
6. G K Chesterton, *The New Jerusalem* (Hodder & Stoughton 1918).

Part Two

The City

Below the spare slopes of the Mount of Olives runs the Valley of Jehosophat, to which the trumpets of the Last Judgement will call the souls of all mankind.... Generations of Christians, Jews and Moslems sleep scattered under a sea of whitened stone, achieving in death in Jerusalem what they had so often failed to achieve in life: a peaceful reconciliation of their claims to its ramparts.

(*O Jerusalem!* Larry Collins & Dominique Lapieroc)

Walk about Zion, go round her,
count her towers,
consider well her ramparts,
view her citadels
that you may tell of them to the next generation.

(Psalm 48:12–13)

O Jerusalem, Jerusalem...how often I have longed to gather your children together...but you were not willing.

(Matthew 23:37).

5

Four Quarters Make One History

> Ten measures of beauty descended to the world.
> Nine were taken by Jerusalem—and one by the
> rest of the world.

So says the Talmud.[1] An exaggeration, but a pardonable one. It can look breathtaking as you drive up over the wooded rocky hummocks of Judaea and suddenly see it, the golden limestone shining, the walls and ramparts in fairytale profusion crowning the shaggy slopes of the highest hill in sight. Or as you slog up the winding track from Jericho and suddenly see three towers stark against the sky, the desert sweeping up to its very skirts. Its heart-stopping quality springs from the fact that its reality so perfectly fits the mental images that have floated in the mind from a Bible-reading childhood.

Jerusalem...Zion...City of God...City of Peace... Eternal City...City of David...Mountain of the Lord... Jerusalem the golden, with milk and honey blest...Lift up your heads, oh ye gates, and be ye lifted up ye everlasting doors...I was glad when they said, Let us go up to the house of the Lord...*What is it about this place?* It has no mineral wealth, supports no industry, boasts no harbour, and stands on no river. Its agriculture is subsistence level, its water-supply totally inadequate, and it sits astride no trade-route. Yet men have fought for it, women wept over it, armies clashed and collided around it. Oaths have been sworn by it, vast pilgrimages undertaken to reach it, crusades launched to capture it. Jews worldwide mark their calenders with events that took place in it. Muslims worldwide are eager to engage in holy wars for or against it. Christians worldwide trace their salvation and hope of heaven to what happened just outside its walls. The adherents of the only three religions in the world that believe in one God, also believe that the last judgement will take place just east of its ramparts. Sophisticated modern Americans in their millions look for world cataclysm around its borders, first foretold three thousand years ago. Christians of all nations in their tens of millions encapsulate their hopes of a new order and a new humanity in terms of a 'new Jerusalem coming down out of heaven from God.'

My first sight of it was from a taxi as we swung down the road from Samaria. The taxi-driver seemed to have picked up his American-English from a 1940's gangster film.

'Wadya make of this guy Josephus?' he asked without any preliminaries, as we lurched into the mainstream traffic. 'Me, I think he's just a traitor, but some reckon he was a patriot and a great guy for puttin' history right.'

I might have been pardoned for thinking he referred to some contemporary politician. In fact he meant Joseph ben Matthias, who Romanised his name to Flavius Josephus. He was born five years after Jesus was crucified, and lived to the year 100. He led the rebel forces in Galilee against the Romans, then changed sides to become the Emperor's confidante and Middle East war correspondent. But Jerusalem is like that. It is so impregnated with its history that people live it, breathe it, argue and sing and write and fight about it. History, glorious and tragic, truthful and mythical, is the Jerusalemite's rationale for every action, his alibi for every misdeed, his argument for being there at all.

Twentieth Century Nazis and Tenth Century Crusaders are all the same to Jerusalem Jews: they came from the same place, and treated Jews the same way. The time between them is telescoped into one period: the time before Jews came back to their mother-city and sent out the message 'Next time you want us, just come and get us.' Jerusalem Jews will point out gleefully that the British Mandate and the United Nations successively chose for their headquarters a place that everyone else for two and a half thousand years had called the Hill of Evil Council! An argument about military strategy is liable to range over the 1982 Lebanon Peace Initiative (sic) and Gideon's campaign against the Midianites. Why not? British General Orde Wingate coached the Haganah (Jewish underground army) from the Book of Judges.

Byzantines and all that

It is all a little confusing to the Christian tourist. The voluble guide waves a hand in the direction of yet another dusty pile of stones and says 'the remains of a Byzantine Church.' The tourist, punch-drunk with undigested facts, wonders whether a Byzantine Church was anything like a Baptist Church. Before he can explore the subject further, he is told, to his surprise, that a Crusader Church was built on top of it (why on top? was it not high enough?). He may even be told, with increasing bewilderment that, of course there was a Constantinian Church underneath it!

Of course, Constantinian, Byzantine and Crusader are not denominational titles like Methodist, Greek Catholic and Marching Church of Zimbabwe with Signs Following (to quote but a few who visit Jerusalem today). Rather they are descriptive of epochs and eras. On the lips of our loquacious guide they are a mixture of historical adjectives (like Bronze Age or Elizabethan) and architectural adjectives (like Renaissance or Gothic). People didn't go around saying 'I'm a Byzantine Christian' or 'I attend a Constantinian Church' any more than people went around describing themselves as Bronze Age Nomads or Gothic Catholics. A church building is Constantinian if it was put up shortly after the Emperor Constantine declared himself and his empire Christian. Byzantine Churches cropped up all over the place when the capital of that same crumbling empire was moved from Rome to Byzantium (Constantinople). Crusader Churches were erected after those most unholy of Christian warriors tore the Holy Land temporarily out of the hands of the Muslims, and built churches everywhere in honour of the Prince of Peace (to celebrate their successful bloodbaths!).

Depressing and unconvincing though the layers of slightly different stone look to the uninstructed, they nevertheless stand for something very moving. They represent faith in Christ and love of his name, stubbornly surviving the vicissitudes of political power struggles, racial tensions and ecclesiastical quarrels. The men and women who prayed and sang in these successive buildings carried on through the generations a love for the name of Jesus, and all it represents, that is recognisable across the chasms of nationality, culture and theology that separate them from us.

The other holocaust

In some cases there is not even a time-gap. In the Armenian Quarter you can step fifteen hundred years back and meet Christians whose churches were ancient in Jerusalem when the Crusaders turned up to 'rescue' them. This unique community gained unenviable fame worldwide this century for a tragic reason. They had their own holocaust, almost thirty years before the Jews had theirs. Armenia in 1916, was a little nation-state sandwiched between Russia and

Turkey. The Turks, embroiled in the First World War, saw Armenians as a threat, for a complex number of national, cultural, political and religious reasons. So they set about the extermination of a race. Close to two million were murdered, either killed in popular pogroms, executed by the authorities, or sent off on impossible overland treks in conditions that guaranteed the death of the elderly, the sick and the young. Their homeland is now indistinguishably shared by Muslim Turkey and Communist Russia. Perhaps six million of them are scattered as international refugees— but some of them came home.

For Armenians had always had another spiritual home. Their land was the first kingdom in the world to declare itself Christian. Evangelised (it is said) by Thaddeus and Bartholomew from the first apostolic band, it had its little persecuted churches from the beginning of the Gentile mission. In the year 301, a convert in the royal family by the name of Gregory was imprisoned and tortured by the king's orders, but subsequently cured that same king of a mysterious disease and saw the whole state from the monarch downwards converted.

The story ever since has been one of successive waves of violence and conquest lapping over the land. Romans, Persians, Arabs, Mongols, Mamelukes—they came and burned and killed and ruled—and went away again. Each time the Armenian survivors came back from the mountains where they had hidden with their national identity, and their Christian faith, intact.

When the Turks began to implement their 'final solution' (24 April 1915 is remembered annually as the Day of Infamy) about twelve hundred of the victims fled to Jerusalem. It was no strange city to Armenians. A list still preserved from the fifth century names seventy of their churches and monasteries in and around Jerusalem. In the tenth and eleventh century a series of Armenian women married successive Crusader kings of Jerusalem and became

their Christian queens. Now, as a world war dragged to an
exhausted halt, as Communist Russia was born, as Britain
promised (irreconcilably) national independence to the
Arabs and a Palestinian homeland to the Jews, the
Armenian Christians made one quarter of biblical Jerusalem
their home. There they preserve the heritage of a vanished
kingdom in the hearts and minds of succeeding generations.

City behind walls

Armenia-in-Jerusalem has its own walls within the city
walls. You have a feeling of intrusion, almost of sacrilege, if
you pluck up enough courage to step under an archway or
push open an ancient door. There is no need to: these timid,
friendly little people are pleased to see you. But the feeling
of secrecy persists. Within these walls are more walls again,
surrounding silent sunlit courtyards. Always just beyond
the corner of your eye and near the limit of your hearing is a
whispering world of scuttling activity. The priests (so many
of them) wear black pointed cowls that cover all of the head
and most of the face, giving a sinister impression which is
unjustified but hard to shake off. Religion, education, social
life and embryonic politics are so closely interwoven that
they are different facets of the same rough-cut stone. The
impression is of one vast monastery, yet twelve hundred
people live here. Property never passes into private hands.
Each family has its own perpetual leasing rights, kept
within the family name. Incidentally every Armenian family
name ends with the letters...ian.

The great deep-throated bell of St James Cathedral
boomed out its call to worship as Rita and I wandered the
courts and exchanged smiles, signals and broken English
with the very occasional passer-by. Behind the shining gold
icons, the hanging censors and gorgeous chandeliers, the
slow sonorous chanting and the incense smoke that catches
eye and throat, is a long-held faith in Christ, expressed in

ways alien to the evangelical Christian. I have no need and no right to measure its reality and depth. But as we dropped into the evangelical coffee-shop on the edge of the Armenian-Quarter where a Muslim Arab and a Jewish yeshivah student had come that day, enquiring the way of salvation in Jesus, we found among the workers an Armenian!

The ruins that rose again

We hurried past the Zion Gate as we had so often before, pausing only to glance at the bulletholes and shell splinters from two wars. A few steps out of the Armenian Quarter took us into astonishingly different world. The Jewish Quarter basked in golden sunshine.

It is a mistake often made by Christians to imagine that Jews only came back in force to Jerusalem in 1967. Only for brief periods have they ever been missing since David the shepherd-king captured it three thousand years ago. They were briefly expelled in 587 BC, but were back within a half-century as their prophets had said they would be. Again in AD 70 they were hounded out by the Romans. Their exile lasted longer that time. Rome tried to erase their memory from the pages of history, renaming Judea 'Palestine' (after their ancient enemies the Philistines) and rebuilding ruined Jerusalem as Aeola Capitolina. From then onwards, a Jewish presence was never more than a few miles away, and slipped back within the walls whenever successive occupies permitted them. Otherwise, Jews throughout the world had to be content to face towards the temple site when they prayed, to greet each other with the pious wish, 'Next year in Jerusalem', and to pray 'May we behold the merciful return to Zion.'

Muslim Arabs were kinder to Jewish Jerusalem than Byzantine Christians had been, and infinitely kinder than Crusaders would prove to be. In 638 the city fell to the Muslims.

When the Caliph Omar visited Jerusalem he asked the Jews: "where would you wish to live in the city?" They answered "In the southern part." Their intention was to be close to the Temple and its gate, as well as the waters of Siloam for ritual bathing. The Emir granted this to them. (Sefer Ha Yishuv)[2]

The 'Jewish Quarter' had come into existence. The contemporary Arab account agrees with the above-quoted Jewish story 'The Jewish community once more flourished, and Jews were among those who guarded the walls of the Dome of the Rock...Jews made the glass and wicks for the oil lamps in Jerusalem from the 8th Century onwards' (Mujir al-Din).[3]

Four centuries later the Crusaders treated Jerusalem Jews abominably, but did not completely expel them. When the Crusaders pulled out, the Jews were back in bigger numbers than ever. In 1187 the Ramban Synagogue went up in the Jewish Quarter; a place of worship until the Jordanians destroyed it in 1948. When the Turks renewed their rule of the city in 1840 there were 5,000 Jews, 4,600 Muslims and 3,300 Christians within the walls. When British General Allenby captured the city from the Turks in 1917 there were 32,000 Jews (three times more numerous than Muslims, eight times more numerous than Christians). Each of these figures had trebled again by 1948 when Israel became a state—thousands of Jews, of course lived in the new sprawling suburbs of East and West Jerusalem, way outside the ancient walls. For the next nineteen years their houses in the Old City were wrecked, their graves desecrated, their synagogues reduced to rubble and their Quarter turned into a rubbish tip.

Whatever the rights and wrongs of the 1967 Six Day War, the Israelis can hardly be accused of coming as alien interlopers with their only argument proceeding from the barrel of a gun. They were coming home. The first thing they had to do was rebuild it. The traditional style has been reproduced. Only one road permits traffic. The rest is all narrow arched lanes, gold-and-green sunlit squares, simple synagogues and flat-roofed houses. The old folk sit in the sun and talk; and the children play in the streets as the prophet said they would.

The wall that was built downwards

There are many wonders to delay the wanderer in the Jewish Quarter, but we were hurrying this day to a private house that epitomises them all. Number 7 Hagitit Street is the home of the Siebenbergs. We had first learned of them through a National Geographical video purchased at Woolworths in the north of England. At one o'clock most afternoons you can call on Theo and Miriam—and have a look at three thousand years of history. Miriam is a 'sabra', born in Israel. Theo hails from Belgium where he made his money with diamonds before fleeing the Nazis. Having dug wealth from the earth (so to speak) he is now putting it back by the million to uncover a different kind of gem. In 1970 the family fulfilled a life ambition and became residents of Jerusalem, purchasing one of the new-built houses in the Jewish Quarter. It stood on a hillock of earth, rock and debris. Seeing the famous Cardo Dig going on only 200 yards away, Theo asked the archaeologists what chance there was of anything significant lying under his house. 'No chance at all', he was told. 'But that doesn't seem right to me,' he replied. 'The Temple was just over there. Why wouldn't Jews have built here then?' 'It's just not on,' was their repeated answer.

He thought it over, talked it over, dreamed about it, until it became an obsession. So he approached architects and engineers. 'What would be the problems if I dug below my floors?' he asked.

They were uniformly horrified. Not only would his own half-million dollar house fall inwards, but the surrounding apartments and houses would slide sideways down the slope. But, continually pestered, the experts grudgingly accepted a theoretical possibility. At a price something like six times the cost of the house, it could be possible to build an immense retaining wall downwards from the surface, held in place by dozens of steel anchors. That was enough. With the help of friends, volunteers, paid workers and a line of donkeys, the Siebenbergs began an eight-year task. The engineers were right; it was possible. But the archaeologists were apparently right too: for two years they found nothing significant. Then there came to light a bronze key ring. No, not a ring to carry keys, but a ring shaped to open locks. The Talmud discusses the thing, and the problem it raises. Can a good Jew wear it on the Sabbath, since it can be regarded as a tool? Their conclusion was—if bronze, no, for it is indeed a tool. If silver, yes, for now it is clearly an ornament: you don't make tools out of silver. A piece of Jewish life and tradition, frozen in time, lay under the Siebenberg's basement.

Now the discoveries came tumbling out. A cistern was dated by a certain-shaped cross on the plaster, until some of the plaster was removed, and revealed stone walls built a hundred years before Christ. Soon its fate became poignantly evident. Layers of black compressed carbon marked its destruction in AD 70, as the triumphant Romans swept into the Upper City, a month after sacking the Temple. Josephus fixes the day for us: 8th Elum, AD 70. A seal of the Tenth Legion confirms that this was indeed, as the records say, the notorious legion that finished the job. Horrible nails, long, thick blunt-headed, only partly rusted, speak grimly of the fate of crucifixion that awaited the terrified inhabitants.

They dug deeper—and struck the line of the famous waterchannel by which Herod piped supplies from 'Solomon's Pools' near Bethlehem, seventeen miles in a straight line, but forty miles by the route it had to follow, pursuing the contours, occasionally crossing a ravine by aqueduct, slowly, slowly descending at an incline of one in a thousand, until at last it reached the Temple. Supplies of water for a quarter of a million animal sacrifices at the great festivals flowed through this brilliant feat of engineering and through the Siebenberg's basement.

They dug further and found a unique glass horn with animal-head decorations, almost unique, at any rate. There are five others known in the world and all are linked with King Mombas, son of Queen Helene of Abilene, who converted with all of her African tribe to Judaism. She was buried north of the city, near the Garden Tomb. He, according to tradition, lived in the Upper City within sight of the Temple. In fact, in the Siebenberg's cellar, it seems.

They dug again. Three storeys down now, and 800 BC. Isaiah's time. The northern kingdom of Israel had fallen to the Assyrians, but good king Hezekiah held out, urged by the prophet to trust in God. Many northern refugees fled to Jerusalem, and for the first time the western hill became a city suburb. It lasted until Jeremiah's time. Then, as that weeping preacher had warned, the terrible Babylonians succeeded where the Assyrians had failed. The Siebenbergs found arrowheads and spearheads from the battle: Rita and I stared at them with awe, and imagined we could hear the clash and shout of fighting.

Ironically, on the same day that some of the arrowheads were found, a rusty but recognisable Czeck sub-machine gun was unearthed, date, 1948. We know who its owner was. The Jews only had two such guns to defend themselves against the onslaught of well equipped Jordanian soldiers. The two owners ran and weaved and dodged and ducked, firing from different positions to give the impression that they were many. Eventually Rizof Mizaki was killed, and the next day the Quarter was evacuated. Sorrowing colleagues threw his gun down a disused cistern—into the Siebenbergs' historical hole-in-the-ground.

So the discoveries went on. Now the dig is complete, Theo and Miriam have installed an exhibition and a slide presentation. They have plans to turn that vast cistern into a musical auditorium. For they found in it an ancient musical instrument, a bronze music-bell. When a choir of young Israelis visited the excavation and stood awed at the bottom of the cistern, they spontaneously began to sing in haunting five-point harmony the psalm, 'Out of the depths I cry unto you Lord'.

We climbed back up to ground-level and talked in the sunshine at the front door. I spoke of including our visit in the book I was writing.

'What is it about?'

'Well—a kind of theological walkabout. I thought of calling it *A Preacher Walks Through the Promised Land*.'

Eyes twinkled. 'I thought someone had done that already—about 1900 years ago!'

He showed me a note in the visitors' book from a fellow Belgian Jew. 'To have saved one soul is to have redeemed the world. To have built one house and revealed all that lies beneath it is to have resurrected our people's tower to the heavens.'

Mosques and Minarets

Take a few steps out of the Jewish into the Arab Quarter and the contrast is dramatic. It is more colourful, more noisy, more crowded, more dirty. The sounds and smells are totally different. The alien chant, half moan and half gargle echoes hauntingly from a score of minarets. Tiny shops, six foot square cubes in crumbling walls, offer their wares as shopkeepers shout and gesticulate and haggle. They look like Ali Baba's forty thieves, but they have a code of honour all their own. Tourists are charged double the expected price and have to reduce it with prolonged argument and counter-offer. Local residents get the goods cheaper; you only have to be introduced once and are then instantly recognised. 'Reedah—you buy theeze,' call out one cheeky proprietor to Rita as she passed the second time. Arabs get a further reduction.

The lanes and alleys are narrow, arched, winding and crowded. Jostling throngs of every conceivable nationality push and heave and scramble. Americans with dark glasses and video cameras, Germans with grotesque nose-shields and cameras, pale-faced English with multicoloured flight-bags, Finns and Italians, Ghanians and Kenyans, Japanese and Philippinos, West Indians and Latin-Americans, many wearing exotic national dress as if to underline that *their* people have really come *here*. Arab head-dresses splash the heaving crowds with black and white or red check, and about one in every fifteen looks uncomfortably like Yasser Arafat. Arab women sport embroidered dresses that tell you (if you have the clue) which village they hail from. Beduin embroidery in cubes and whorls tells those who can interpret the family history in symbols: births, marriages and deaths for a couple of centuries. Some of the women crouch on any available step, a handful of herbs or a basketful of fruit for sale.

And there are priests everywhere. Varieties of Christianity unknown to British or American evangelicals make their bid for attention in the exotic diversity of colour and shape of their head-dresses. Jews seem quite at home, too. Sweeping self-consciously down the short-cut to the Wall, they flaunt their swashbuckling prayer-shawls, huge bobbing fur hats proclaim Russia as the country of origin for some, and multi-coloured turbans topping white robes proclaim Ethiopa as the home of others. What exactly *is* a Jew, one wonders again, when he can be black African, brown Yemeni, black-bearded Polish or red-faced American?

Golden dome and silver sanctuary

The glory of the Arab Quarter is the gigantic Dome of the
Rock, called the Mosque of Omar. It is an enormous shrine,
not for corporate acts of worship but for individual visitors
of any race and creed. (as long as you remove your shoes
and it isn't Friday).

Its dimensions are awesome, its golden dome magnificent,
its myriad multi-coloured mosaics breathtaking. Just why
it is there is not clear. For centuries Jewish tradition identified the rock that thrusts through its floor as the summit of
the mountain—and the mountain of Moriah where Abraham almost sacrificed Isaac. It is a nice thought, for in this
general area Solomon's temple later stood. But on what
biblical or historical grounds the two places are identified
as one, I cannot discover. When the world was thought to
be a flat disc, this area was considered the centre. Another
nice thought, but not one likely to increase my confidence in
tradition.

When Caliph Omar conquered the city in 638, he did
erect a mosque, but this was not it. The silver-topped Aksa
mosque was built nearby, on the same flat platform of rock
originally laid by Herod's workmen. It is the third most
holy site of Islam, after Mecca and Medina. Respectful
though Muslims were of Abraham and Isaac, something a
little more Islamic was felt to be necessary. So Ishmael the
Arab neatly replaced Isaac the Jew in the biblical story.
And for good measure it was suggested that Mohammed,
who undoubtedly visited the city, here mounted a magical
horse at this spot and thence rode to heaven. The mark left
by the sole of his foot will be shown to you on request. Islam
is never slow to invent, imitate and improvise.

The entire Temple Mount platform is called Haram
el-Shariff (the Noble Sanctuary). Its atmosphere is palpable,
unique, slightly frightening. Devout Jews refuse to put a foot
in the whole area, for fear of inadvertently treading where

the Holy of Holies once stood, forbidden to any but the High Priest once a year. It is by no means certain that the floor of the Dome marks the exact spot. Complicated calculations recently carried out suggest that a point 150 yards north of the Dome is the right place. The tiny Dome of the Tablets is in direct line with the Golden Gate, the ancient entry which stood directly opposite the Altar of Burnt Offering and the door of the Sanctuary. This suggestion had caused a good deal of embarrassment to the Arabs and a quiver of excitement to those Jews and Christians whose prophetic scenario includes a rebuilding of the Temple. Walk anywhere near the Dome of the Tablets nowadays and you will get suspicious looks and a curt wave of dismissal from the Waqf (Islamic guards). Display a camera or a tape-measure and you are likely to get run off. I managed a quick snap by standing with my back to it and employing some deft and surreptitious gymnastics.

On Fridays the whole area is one mass of multicoloured head-dresses and trouser suits as uncountable thousands pour up the steps and through the arches to stand, kneel and prostrate themselves in prayer. On other days visitors are cautiously welcome if they keep the rules. Reveal bare arms or legs (men or women) and you will be forcefully enveloped in a pale blue piece of shapeless material smelling of goodness knows what and stained with sweat. Men and women must not hold hands here. A young couple near me were curtly forbidden to do it. Having no idea of the language they nervously clung to each other, only to be violently harangued. A whispered explanation defused the situation, and the guard marched off with a snarl.

The atmosphere is often tense. Christian tourists want to see it, but shrink from it. Some of them seriously regard the Dome as 'the abomination that causes desolation, standing in the holy place' (Daniel 11:31 and Matthew 24:15). I understand their concern, but question their theology and their history.

Arab feeling soon runs high here, and is expressed in anti-Christian and anti-Jewish frenzy. Mullahs shouting over the minarets' loud-speakers can turn a congregation into a rampaging mob within minutes. As I write, I watch on the TV screen Israeli soldiers dispersing one such mob with tear-gas and four-foot truncheons whilst snipers deploy around the walls (mercifully they do not fire). In 1969 the mosque was mysteriously arsonised, and Arabs will earnestly assure you that the Jerusalem fire service took two hours to respond. Incidents in more recent years breathe fanaticism and imbalance. A demented Australian Christian tossed hand-grenades to speed the Dome's demolition and hasten the rebuilding of the Temple. An American-Israeli soldier went out of his mind and opened fire on worshippers with a machinegun. A Jewish terrorist group were caught trying to dynamite the mosque (with magnificent impartiality their colleagues planted hand-grenades in Muslim prayer-rooms and Catholic churches, and set the Baptist Chapel in West Jerusalem on fire). Religion, politics and racialism form a heady and dangerous mix in the Noble Sanctuary.

Notes

1. Talmud, *Kiddushim*, 49b.
2. Sefer Ha Yishuv, 'Getting Jerusalem Together' (Fran Albert, Archaeological Seminar Ltd, 1984), p 32.
3. Mujir al-Din, 'History of Jerusalem and Hebron' Quoted from *Getting Jerusalem Together* p 33.

6

Behold the Wondrous Cross

Turn at rightangles from the Arab shops and soukhs, dive down some steps, and you are in a different world. The Christian Quarter of the old city welcomes you.

It is still very Arabic: it always comes as something of a shock to discover that Arabs may well be Christians. Bishop Kafiti of St George's Anglican Cathedral feels sore about that. 'Christians come from Europe and America on pilgrimage, and never meet an indigenous Christian, visit an Arab congregation, or show any awareness of the ancient church of the Middle East,' he complained to me once.

Even the street names have an ecclesiastical ring: like Great Patriarchate Street, reminding us that an Arab Christian is most likely to be Greek Orthodox if he is not Roman Catholic.

And now a few twists and turns, and you are outside the Church of the Holy Sepulchre. Here is the central shrine of Christendom. This place was to bloodthirsty, land-hungry but oddly pious Crusaders, what the golden fleece was to Jason and the holy grail to King Arthur's Knights. The vast, rambling, echoing edifice leaves many modern Christians uneasy, bewildered and disillusioned. The first time I accidentally wandered in, I fled within minutes. A greasy character, some lower order of ecclesiastic, approached me with the mien of an Egyptian selling doubtful postcards. For so many shekels, he whispered, he would—what? I wasn't sure.

A bearded face peered out from a parted curtain covering some crevice in the wall, and offered me a candle, at a price. The sharp sickly smell of incense filled the porticoed gloom and a dolorous chanting echoed through the smoke. Clanking chains suitable to adorn skeletons in dungeons festooned the ceilings with swinging censors. That was enough.

Since then, I've dutifully forced myself to return to this morbid shrine and explore the reeking history which it enfolds. Without doubt great events have happened here, great piety has been displayed here, and great lunacies have been perpetrated here. People have walked for a year to get here and kiss its stones. The Crusaders marched here to set the blood of Arabs and Jews running ankle-deep in the lanes around, and to reclaim it in triumph for the Prince of Peace.

Did Jesus really die and rise again in the area of those vast rambling halls? Certainly Christians for fifteen hundred years have thought so. One's first reaction is, 'this can't be the place!' Examination of the evidence brings me to 'I hope it isn't the place!' Those who are eventually and reluctantly convinced, tend to say 'Well it figures! They crucified him then, and they're killing all he stands for now.' That may well be grossly unfair. I just don't know. Rational thought is difficult here.

A piece of detection

Putting together the alleged evidence is a confusing business. Tantalising hints abound. False clues clamour. One thing is clear. When Constantine became the first Christian Roman Emperor, his mother Helena visited the Holy Land in search of places of which it could be said, here it happened. The Mount of Olives was no problem, and Bethlehem provided few puzzles, but Jerusalem had been completely levelled and rebuilt by Hadrian a hundred years after the foundation of the Church and almost two hundred years before Helena arrived. Whatever she found, whatever reasoning she pursued, within a short while she had the emperor's funds and a site for the erection of a lavish building to commemorate the death and resurrection of Jesus.

Eusebius, writing in 336, shortly after the event, describes with gusto the discovery of the site.

> As one layer after another was laid bare, the place beneath the earth appeared. Then forthwith, contrary to all expectation, did the venerable and hallowed monument of our Saviour's resurrection become visible, and the most holy cave received what was an exact emblem of His coming to life.... No power of language seems worthy to describe the wonder.... The token of that most holy passion, long ago buried underground (had) remained unknown for so many cycles of years, until it should shine forth to His servants.[1]

Purple passages abound in Eusebius: it is difficult to distinguish facts from eloquence.

So the site was unknown. How was it found? One version says Helena was 'divinely directed by dreams.'[2] Another says a nameless Jew 'derived his information from some documents come to him by paternal inheritance' and then, with disarming naivete adds, 'but it seems more accordant with truth to suppose that God revealed the fact by means of signs and dreams.'[3]

This revealing quotation comes perhaps a hundred years after the event. A century later the story has gained some nice circumstantial details.

The Empress, *it is said*, had a divine vision. The Bishop, when he heard, went out to meet her accompanied by his suffragan bishops. *When all were at a loss* what to do, and each suggested a different thing, acting on *mere conjecture*, Bishop Macarius bade them all to be of a quiet mind and offer heartfelt prayers to God. When this was done the place was *miraculously revealed* to the Bishop, being that wherein the figure of the most unclean goddess stood.[4] (Italics mine)

The 'unclean goddess' was Venus. The version usually related nowadays explains that the Emperor Hadrian, in order to insult the Christian, had built a temple to Venus on the known site of the crucifixion, thus inadvertently preserving the memory of the very thing which he wished to obliterate. This is not unlikely; Hadrian almost certainly did something similar at Bethlehem and unwittingly preserved Christ's birthplace.

But in that case, there would have been no difficulty in *finding* the place. They simply had to demolish the pagan temple, as they did in Bethlehem. So why the ignorance, the mystery, the search, and the need for miraculous disclosures?

The story goes on being embroidered as years pass. Helena found not only the hill of Calvary and the tomb, but the three crosses (Christ's and the two thieves) buried nearby in a water cistern. You will be shown what purports to be the cistern today, deep under the church, its walls entirely covered with little carved crosses where pilgrims have left their marks from far-off countries. But the story is an absurdity. The wood could not have been preserved. The crosses could not have been identified and kept in the first place: crosses were used and re-used for a succession of victims. Most serious of all, a complete cross was not something that was moved. The upward stem would simply be a standing tree (the New Testament repeatedly says it was: Acts 5:30, Acts 10:39, Acts 13:29, Galations 3:13, 1 Peter 2:24). The cross-piece alone was mobile. It was carried through the streets by the victim, with the accusation nailed to it. It was *this* that Jesus, after two beatings, was unable to carry.

So the story meanders on. What becomes clear is that Bishop Macarius very much wanted money for a new church, and Helena very much wanted to find the sites of biblical events. The contemplation of some of the characteristics of Roman and Byzantine church power-struggles is not an exercise calculated to increase confidence in the facts and the motives involved in erecting a lavish and luxurious shrine to the Saviour's suffering.

However, erect it they did—and in the process effectively ruined any chance of preserving evidence in support of the site's choice.

The hill of Calvary was actually cut back to one thirty-foot cube of rock and then overlaid with marble. The nearby tomb-area was similarly treated; most of the rocky hillside cut away leaving one hollow cube which was then carved into lavish shapes and decorated. A huge domed basilica was then built over both areas. Later the tomb was completely destroyed by ravaging Persians (the church at Bethlehem was the only one that escaped their destruction. It contained a painting of the Wise Men worshiping the infant Jesus. The magi were portrayed as *Persians*. The invaders were so gratified that they spared the church.).

The present erection which is pointed out as the tomb of Christ, in no way fits the Gospel narrative, and is owned by one oriental group. There is a tiny alternative tomb tacked on the back by a rival hierarchy. Altogether five churches stake their claim to the shrine—Greek Orthodox, Roman Catholic, Syrian Jacobite, Armenian and Coptic. Interminable arguments rage over who owns what. For centuries two Muslim families have kept the keys, to keep warring factions apart and punch-ups to a minimum. The unfortunate Ethiopians have been expelled by their co-religionists, and live in mud huts on the roof.

Visually, the Holy Sepulchre offers nothing. There is no

execution-hill, no garden, no road where passers mocked, no rolling-stone tomb, no ledge on which the body lay. It is well inside the city wall in a heavily built-up area. If the wall in Jesus' time was really much further in to the south (as advocates of the Holy Sepulchre have to assert) then the site might just have been barely outside, as both Bible account and Roman custom demand. That puts the wall along a hypothetical line that would make it virtually indefensible, with higher ground dominating it from the outside.

It is all just possible. A hundred years before Christ, the wall was much further in, that is certain. The area was at one time a burial ground outside the city. I once clambered behind a piece of broken wall (left unrepaired for decades by quarrelling ecclesiastics fearful of acceding 'rights' to rival sects) and found myself in an eerie area which archaeologists have since told me was an ancient quarry. Several *khokhim* (oven-like graves) penetrate the sides of the quarry. This was the commonest form of burial. But Jesus was quite specifically *not* buried in such a grave, rather in a wealthy man's sepulchre (a vaulted tomb). The Gospel account infers one solitary private burial-chamber in a private garden, not a well used public burial-ground in a quarry (see Luke 23:50–53).

In the long run, the Holy Sepulchre's most impressive argument is simply that it is there. It has been there a very long time. Most Christians throughout most of history have assumed it is the very place. A vast volume of devotion, worship, contemplation and passion has focused on this spot. I shall take the reader to a place that appeals to me more and which offers a visual impact impossible in this dusty crowded mausoleum. But even this place falls tauntingly short of offering decisive and final evidence. Perhaps God wants it that way. For the *fact* of Christ's death and resurrection is totally central to Christianity, but the *place* is of no vital consequence. In that death and rising, God was acting decisively for the world's salvation and for mine.

That is where faith takes its stand, love gathers its energy and worship finds its motive.

I watch a woman thinly clad, her face lined with age and care. She kneels over the stone that supposedly marks the place where Jesus' body was brought down from the cross for anointing.

She repeatedly kisses the stone with rapt gaze. Idolatory? No—why should it be that? Who but the Holy Spirit can give her such love for the Saviour? What but the reality of his suffering for her (wherever it happened) can give her relief and peace? A black-robed priest intones a chant in the supposed place where the cross was laid to take its sacred burden. I know him. As a teenager in far-off Greece he became possessed of a desire above all else to live and pray at the place where Jesus died. His parents tried to dissuade him, and he threatened to run away. Years of intensive training followed. Now he lives out his days and years, caught up in a pageant of cyclic praise and meditation which is foreign to my inclination and experience but in which I can recognise a man touching the eternal. Can anyone doubt that the love of Christ constrains him?

Gordon's Calvary

My first view of the rival Calvary-site was as accidental as my first sight of the Holy Sepulchre. Four of us were getting to know Jerusalem for the first time, and without the assistance of a professional guide we were making a singular muddle of it. One of my friends grabbed my arm as we wandered through the archways of the Damascus Gate and found ourselves outside the walls in Arab Jerusalem. 'Look —shape of a skull! It *must* be!' We dodged hooting buses in the crowded bus-terminus and stood below a forty foot cliff gazing upwards. Varigated limestone made odd shapes where erosion had worn away the softer stone and left the harder. Calvary. Golgotha. Roman and Hebrew for *skull*.

Could this be where Jesus died? If it was, where was the garden? John tells us 'Carrying his own cross, he went out to the Place of the Skull. Here they crucified him. ... At the place where Jesus was crucified, there was a garden and in the garden a new tomb...they laid Jesus there' (John 19:17,41 & 42).

We had all heard vaguely of the Garden Tomb beside Gordon's Calvary. I recalled a hero-preacher from my teens, a chaplain with the Mission to Mediterranean Garrisons, with tales of serving soldiers whom he'd introduced to Jesus at that place.

Excited questions of everyone within reach elicited indifferent shrugs and curt denials. No one, it seemed, had heard of the place. 'If it *is* the spot, they still treat it the same,' I commented. 'Is it nothing to you, all ye that pass by?'

Eventually, with help from a map, we did three right-turns through crowded streets, and found a doorway through a high wall which brought us back to the hill at a higher level. Inside the doorway a garden of astonishing greenery beckoned us. The Garden Tomb. There was bustle everywhere. Paths zig-zagged amongst the flowers below the giant Jerusalem pines, amongst the palms and pomegranets. Groups of tourists filled every path. Somewhere in the near-distance voices were lifted in song—two songs— no, three, and in different languages. A blonde young man with Scandinavian accent offered to show us round. He quoted the Bible with simple conviction. He spoke of Jesus, as of a personal friend.

We found ourselves on a viewing platform above the bus-station, gazing across at Skull Hill again. Yes—two eye-sockets, a suggestion of a nose, even a few broken teeth. The guide explained.

This is undoubtedly an ancient Jewish execution site. Bet-ha-Sekilah (one of its names) means Place of Stoning. Execution was carried out, according to the Talmud, by

casting the victim down from a cliff top and dropping a
boulder from the height on to his chest. Appointed men
called the witnesses performed this task. Hopefully, the first
fall killed him, but afterwards the general public could join
in with rocks and stones to complete the job. Of Stephen's
martyrdom we read, 'They began to stone him. Meanwhile
the witnesses laid their clothes at the feet of a young man
named Saul' (Acts 7:58).

Eusebius, the church historian, describes the stoning of
James the Just, leader of the Jerusalem Church and Jesus'
brother,

> Accordingly they went up and *cast the Just down*. They said to
> one another, 'Let us stone James the Just,' and they began to
> stone him. *Since he was not killed by the fall*, he turned and knelt
> down saying, 'I beseech thee Lord God Father, forgive them for
> they know not what they do.'[5]

Our guide went on to reason that the most likely place for
the Romans to carry out their form of execution was in an
already-used Jewish execution site. It seems likely. The
crosses would already stand there, needing only the grim
cross-piece carried to the site by the condemned victims.
For Jewish law required the bodies of stoned criminals to be
hanged or displayed on poles or trees afterwards, so that all
might witness the completion of the sentence. Deuteronomy
describes this, and Paul writing to the Galatians links the
custom and its significance with the cross of Christ, in
astonishing words that go right to the heart of the gospel.
'Christ redeemed us from the curse of the law by becoming
a curse for us, for it is written: "Cursed is everyone who is
hanged on a tree".' (Gal 3:13, Deut 21:23)

The guide was a sensitive young man, with a love for
Christ that shone on his face (incidentally, although I later
went to live and work at the Garden, I could never discover
who he was. There were no records of any of the staff being
as young as he was, and long-standing workers there denied

any knowledge of him. Do some angels have Scandinavian accents, I wonder?) He offered no guarantees. This *may* be the place. It fits the description in every detail. It provides a visual aid. It throws light on some of the puzzling details. Most of all, it turns our attention to Jesus. Why did He die? Just over there (pointing) lies the temple mount. On its slopes tens of thousands of sacrifices have been offered that could no more than hopefully *symbolise* the taking away of sin. But Jesus offered one sacrifice for sin—once and for all—and the work was done. Reality. Pardon. New beginnings.

Rita and I held hands and quietly wept. It was one of those spiritual experiences that sometimes come unbidden, and form no necessary part of the life of faith but are welcome bonuses of grace. We offered ourselves again to the service of Christ, wherever that might take us. We offered our sons and their children to come. Not in our wildest dreams did we imagine that part of God's acceptance of our offer would be to send us back to live in this place and occupy an open-air pulpit beside an empty tomb from which we would share his grace with international thousands.

Cross and controversy

The Garden Tomb leaves few people unmoved, though reactions vary to extremes. I know Christian leaders (usually American) who hold to its authenticity as an article of faith. Mormons claim to have a personal revelation about it. Judging by other Mormon 'revelations', that to me is a strong argument against it! Pentecostalists have sometimes told me, 'As soon as I entered, the Spirit told me this is the place.' I know the feeling, but would prefer to say 'my spirit' rather than 'the Spirit'. Others see it as an attack on traditional Christianity, an insult, a red flag waved to the bull of religious controversy. Some local high-church

Anglicans refer to it disparagingly as Disneyland. Many
Roman Catholics love it and affirm that although the Holy
Sepulchre is *the* place the Garden Tomb 'feels right', and is
more conducive to worship. As a general rule the more
Western, the more Protestant, the more Conservative
Evangelical people are, the more they favour the Garden
Tomb.

The Garden Tomb Association themselves make modest
claims. Their little illustrated brochure, which sells in
thousands, simply describes it as a Herodian tomb in an
area regarded by many people as the garden of Joseph of
Arimathaea. The Association acts as trustees for land
originally bought by Archbishop Benson of Canterbury in
1880. The story is a fascinating one.

In 1867 the Greek owner of this area, encouraged by
certain clues, began to dig in search of a possible water
cistern. It was there to be found, but he dug in the wrong
place and discovered instead what he took to be an old cave.
He put it into use as a garden shed, but the garden never
came into being for the hoped-for water cistern remained
hidden. Along came a German archaeologist and philan-
thropist, called Conrad Schick. What he saw excited him.
'This,' he said, 'is a tomb from the Herodian period.'
Several explorers were unimpressed at this time by the
claims of the Holy Sepulchre, and at least two other tombs
north of the present city wall were regarded as possibilities
for the tomb of Jesus.

Interest lapsed—until General ('Chinese') Gordon came
on the scene. This extraordinary Victorian hero, adventurer,
and Christian soldier, was on his way to Khartoum where
his destiny awaited him. He stayed with friends whose
house stood on the northern city wall, beside the old Roman
road, and opposite what now has become the bus-station.
According to legend, he noticed the hill's resemblance to a
skull, and pronounced it to be Calvary, although that is a
shorthand version. In actual fact he came with his calcula-

tions already made and his conclusions already reached. His thinking was based on a complicated 'typology' much in vogue at that time, which saw detailed symbolic and prophetic significance in every detail of Old Testament ritual. To Gordon, Calvary had to be north of the Temple Mount, and the skull must be part of a crucifixion figure as viewed from above the city. His reasoning is something of an embarrassment nowadays. Nevertheless, the hill *does* look like a skull, and Gordon *did* point it out, and everyone suddenly recalled that five minutes walk away was a Herodian tomb.

The General went off to his martyrdom and into the pages of popular history. His letter home describing Skull Hill created a sensation. A full excavation of the neglected tomb was launched, and results were startling. Most tombs are natural caves, but this is carved out of rock—as the Bible describes (Mat 27:60). Rolling-stone tombs are rare, but this one has a channel cut across the floor in front of the door which may well have been the runner for such a stone (again Matthew 27:60). It has two chambers: one for burial and the other for mourners to watch and weep before interment. Several Gospel incidents make it clear that a space such as this must have existed. (eg Luke 24:2–3). The design is unusual, with the burial chamber on the right inside the door, instead of beyond the weeping-chamber— but this is how Mark describes it (Mark 16:5). John vividly relates how, on Easter morning, he hesitated to step inside, but peered in from the doorway and could see from that position the winding-cloths lying discarded (Jn 20:3–5). To look in this way would be impossible in any other known tomb in Jerusalem, but is exactly appropriate of the Garden Tomb. One of the most impressive and eerie moments for any visitor is to imitate John's movements and see how they correspond to the Gospel account.

There are several evidences of early Christian use of the tomb as some kind of shrine. The position in relation to

Skull Hill is correct (if indeed Skull Hill is Calvary). And that elusive water-cistern turned up in a later excavation. It is massive—the size of a parish church—yet carved out of solid rock to store one quarter million gallons of rainwater, thus making a garden possible (Jn 19:41). Later still a splendidly preserved wine-press was found. Both date from the correct period.

Visually, the whole thing is perfect. Archaeologically, the case is not as overwhelming as it seems, and historically it is weak. Does it really matter? Not a bit.

The *historical* fact that Jesus was crucified in the circumstances related in the Bible is so overwhelmingly clear that one could only question or deny it if one's mind were already darkened by the wish that it had never happened. The *theological* meaning depends on factors totally outside historical and archaeological proof. Only the Spirit of God can teach a man or woman to say, 'He loved me and gave himself for me.' The geographical location has nothing to do with either. To be able to point to a spot of earth and say 'He died here' is no step at all towards saying 'He died for me.' *That* is the cry of faith.

As a visual aid to the essential Gospel story, the Garden Tomb is as superb as the Holy Sepulchre is abysmal. But that comment is quite subjective. Some people are as moved by candles and incense, crumbling stones and chanting priests, as I am by a rocky hill, a garden of greenery and a rock-hewn tomb. What matters is that we take our place, with penitence, faith and adoration, at the foot of a cross which does not now stand on a square yard of Palestinian soil, but towers over a suffering, sinning world with the offer of pardon and peace with God.

I have a colourful imagination when awake, and dream technicolor dreams of mystifying complexity when I sleep. But never, waking or sleeping, did I dream the first ten times I visted Gordon's Calvary and the Garden Tomb that for sixteen unforgettable months they would constitute my home and my church. There we saw what successive chaplains, directors, chairmen and guides have seen since it was opened to the public in 1895.

Men and women from a bewildering variety of nations came and looked and listened—and found faith restored or newly created, in the Garden.

For the tomb is empty. Wherever the authentic grave is, it housed its precious guest for only parts of three days. Then Jesus rose and went. He did not leave it totally empty. The grave-clothes, still wrapped and interleaved with spices, lay abandoned. No grave-robbers had unwrapped them. The body came *through* them, as it came through the stone and through closed doors (the rolling stone was not moved to let him out: how could it keep him in? It was moved to allow the disciples in, to discover that Christ had risen!). And a small significant detail: the headcloth lay folded in a place of its own (Jn 20:3–7). Jesus was a carpenter. When a craftsman in his time had finished a task for his customer, he washed his hands on a napkin, folded it and left it beside the finished task. The symbolic message was 'job done'.

And so it was—gloriously and completely. 'Jesus said, "It is finished". With that he bowed his head and gave up his spirit.' (Jn 19:30).

> Lifted up was He to die,
> 'It is finished' was His cry,
> Now in Heaven exalted high,
> Hallelujah, what a Saviour.[6]

Notes

1.   Eusebius, *Life of Constantine* Chapter 3:28–30.
2.   Socrates, *Historia Ecclesiastica* Chapter 1:17.
3.   Sozomen, *Historia Ecclesiastica* Chapter 2:1.
4.   Alexander Monachus, *The Invention of the Holy Cross*.

5. Eusebius, Ecclesiastical History 2:23. Josephus also briefly records the event, and dates it as AD 61. (Josephus, *Antiquities of the Jews* 20:9–1).
6. Philip Bliss, the hymn, 'Man of Sorrows'.

7

The Stones Cry Out

The two of us edged forward, crouched behind bushes, until we were close enough to peer through the barbed wire. The fighting had stopped for the moment. Soldiers and police lounged about, students sat on the lips of the trenches, black-coated demonstrators seethed and heaved and mustered at the corner of the road but kept their distance.

No, it was not a revolution. It was the King David Dig. The trenches were archaeological excavations, the students were working for the university, and the demonstrators were the Jewish religious *hassidim* trying to stop them. The barbed wire was to keep both sides away, for the moment, from a mysterious half-revealed rounded stone erection, rather like one segment of an immense stone beehive. This was archaeology in Jerusalem, fraught with controversy, frustrated by high feeling, bogged down in another science-versus-religion wrangle.

South-west of the Temple Mount, and well outside the southern city wall a ridge of rock and earth thrusts into the Kedron Valley. A few Arab houses perch on the summit, its sides too steeply slanted for much building. As is the way with Middle Eastern cities, it had become a rubbish dump, until the Hebrew University followed up some half-forgotten clues from a century ago and resurrected a contentious theory—the *real* Jerusalem, the original place, the city of David, they suggested, was right here.

Two typical Victorian characters started it all. Lt Charles Warren, a Richard Hannay kind of figure, aided by his indefatigable adjutant Corporal Birtles, came to Turkish Jerusalem in 1867. They carried a commission from the Palestine Exploration Fund (patron, Queen Victoria). The English had a mammoth task. Against the constant opposition and obstacles of the corrupt Turkish authorities they had to reconstruct as best they could the topography of the original Bible city. This they assumed, of course, to be underneath the present city, as indeed it proved to have been from about Isaiah's time onwards.

The soldiers' method was unique and hair-raising. To attract as little attention as possible, they dug deep vertical shafts (in some places 130 feet down through the rubble of centuries) until they reached bedrock. At the bottom of the shafts they branched out in horizontal tunnels. Several times they were nearly killed. As Warren put it in his modest English manner, 'Necessity obliged us to overstep the bounds of caution.' They had no scientific way of dating any finds, but their meticulous records preserved hundreds of facts that became the basis for later discoveries and revelations.

Like this one. Beavering away at the bottom of a shaft beside the southwest corner of the Temple Mount, they found remains of a massive outer wall—hundres of feet *outside* the city, and pointing, in fact, towards the Gihon Spring down in the valley, the only natural water supply that outlasted the winter rains. Everyone was already vaguely aware of a man-made tunnel that plunged from this spring into the mountain-side and apparently re-appeared a mile away at the other side of the ridge, as the Pool of Siloam, mentioned in the Bible (Neh 3:15, Jn 9:7–11).

Captain Warren (as he had now become) waded through the half-blocked tunnel, water sometimes up to his chin and the roof inches above his head, and discovered another oddity. A chimney-like shaft opened up above his head, soaring into the blackness above. It was irresistable. Captain and Sergeant (Birtles too had got his promotion) performed a remarkable feat of highly dangerous mountaineering, heaving and scrambling and wedging their way upwards through shafts and ledges and caves, and emerged in daylight two-thirds of the way up the ridge. Warren did some hard thinking. The horizontal tunnel right through the ridge could be the one referred to by Isaiah in the Bible. Threatened by the invading Assyrians, good king Hezekiah prepared for siege, and piped the spring-water that was outside the walls through the mountain and into the city. 'Hezekiah made the pool and the tunnel by which he brought water into the city' (2 Kings 20:20). He consulted with his officials and military staff about blocking off the water from the springs outside the city: 'Why should the Kings of Assyria come and find plenty of water?' (2 Chron 32:3–5).

The trouble was, the Pool of Siloam at the receiving end was still well outside the walls. It was absurd. Unless the town walls had once been down in the valley! Warren had guessed correctly. Twelve years later children venturing into the tunnel from the lower end, found an ancient Hebrew inscription marking the point where Hezekiah's diggers, working from both ends, met in the middle. It must have been a dramatic moment, and the inscription does justice to the event.

Axe to axe they cut, each man towards his fellow. While there were yet three cubits to be cut through, the voice of one man calling to the other was heard. When the tunnel was driven through, the excavators met man to man, pick to pick, and the water flowed for 1,200 cubits from the spring to the resevoir.[1]

Secret water supply

So much for the horizontal channel now known to thousands of tourists as Hezekiah's Tunnel. What about the *vertical* tunnel? There was another mysterious Scripture to follow up, a far older one. When David and his troops first came to Jerusalem it was the Citadel of the Jebusites, a pagan enclave in the middle of the disorganised clans of Israel. Secure in their fortress the Jebusites taunted all intruders and claimed that their invalids could defend the walls against attack.

> "Even the blind and the lame can ward you off," they thought. Nevertheless, David captured the fortress of Zion. He said, "Anyone who conquers the Jebusites will have to use the water shaft." He took up residence in the fortress and called it the City of David. He built up the area around, from the supporting terraces around (2 Sam 5:6−9).

The pieces were coming together for Captain Warren. Long before the cutting of Hezekiah's tunnel, the Jebusites, it seemed, had their own device for withstanding siege with their water supply outside. They covered the mouth of the underground spring, cut a subterranean canal a hundred yards horizontally, and then cut a vertical tunnel down to it from high above. Ropes and wooden buckets would do the rest. Thereby they secured water for everyone inside whilst the enemy camped outside and did without, until David turned the tables, discovered the shaft, sent his commandos up it and broke into the city. The water-shaft had become a Trojan horse.

All of this could only mean one thing. David's city was on the south-west ridge, outside the later Jerusalem of Jesus' time.

'Out of the question' affirmed the scholars to whom Captain Warren reported. True enough, the Book of Nehemiah gave the same impression. Carefully analyse the governor's famous moonlit reconnaissance (Neh 2:13−16) and you get the impression that the old city whose ruins he surveyed was on the slopes of the valley, not on top. Moreover, you discover why that reformer built it further north on the hilltop—the debris of destruction choked the valley, and it was easier to start again further up. Nehemiah's decision unwittingly preserved David's city under a shield of earth and rubble for 2,400 years, until it could be scientifically explored.

Unfortunately for Captain Warren, religious controversy broke out just as he reported his finds. Catholic and Orthodox authorities were scandalised at questions being raised over their traditional 'holy sites'. That same year the Garden Tomb was discovered as a possible alternative to the Church of the Holy Sepulchre. The whole thing was clearly a Protestant plot. Warren's Shaft was named after the intrepid climber (who preserved his reputation by climbing the Rock of Gibraltar)—and promptly forgotten.

Religious controversy also plagued the resumption of the quest a hundred years later. By then a galaxy of names had added their contributions: Bromislow Parker, Pere Hugues Vincent, Macalister, and the redoubtable British pioneer Dame Kathleen Kenyon (Arabs will stop you in the Kedron Valley today and try to sell you old coins which they say they found whilst working for 'Ken Yon'). All had given weight to the assertion that David's capital was under that rubbish dump.

The City of David Society was formed, and one of Israel's top archaeologists, Dr Yigal Shiloh gathered professionals and volunteers from all over the world. The ultra-orthodox Jews suddenly objected. The area, they announced, was an ancient cemetery, and the disturbing of the dead is a particularly nasty offence to Jewish piety. No evidence of burial-plots was ever found, but tempers boiled over. *Hassidim* in their black frock-coats and homburg hats stoned the excavators, leaped into the trenches, prostrated themselves over the discoveries, struggled with the students and the police, and organised protest demos.

The diggers dug doggedly on and found, amongst other things, that stone beehive structure. Rumours and speculation flew. It was King David's tomb. It was part of a pyramid. Its pyramidal shape suggested that it was built by Solomon for his Egyptian princess. It was a vault guarding fabulous treasure. No wonder one of my church deacons and I were creeping up to the barbed wire to have a peek. After all, we were temporary students at the Hebrew University, and our course was 'Jerusalem Through The Ages'.

The truth was rather less dramatic, but still gratifying: the structure was solid. It is the retaining wall on which the Jebusite citadel presumably stood—a little like one of those squat square fortresses whose ruins add poignancy to the Scottish coastline. It became David's citadel. In the most limited sense of that emotive word, it is Zion.

The Bible comes to life

Eight years of digging, clearing and shifting have followed, and the excavation is complete, with part of the area laid out as an archaeological garden with walkways and explanatory signs. Only three small areas have been exposed, but they are dramatic enough. To have found the citadel itself was a marvellous success. The walls that made the Jebusites so confident are reconstructed in part. The caves at the top end of Warren's Shaft house a tiny museum. Beside the citadel wall are houses destroyed in the tragic climax of judgement when in 586 BC Babylonians over-ran Jerusalem as Jeremiah the weeping prophet had foretold. Arrowheads bear grim witness to the fighting; charred beams and carbonised furniture to its outcome. 'Nebuzaradan, commander of the imperial guard of Nebuchadnezzar King of Babylon came to Jerusalem...Every important building he burned down...and carried into exile the people that remained' (2 Kings 25:8–11).

In one of the houses the awesome discovery was made. A *bulla* is a kind of signet-ring, shaped in stone on which a man's autograph or personal mark was pressed on to the wax seal of a closed 'book' (a *megilla* or scroll). Jeremiah 2:9–15 gives an example of its use incidentally. In what was clearly an administrative office near the citadel, fifty *bullae* were found. Each bears an inscription 'belonging to…' and a personal name. Three of them are of people who appear together in one Bible story.

The prophet Jeremiah dictates to his scribe Baruch warnings of divine judgement, to be read aloud to the King. The nervous officials oblige, and the scene is set as the King was sitting in the winter apartment, with a fire burning in the firepot in front of him. He didn't like what he heard, and in grim silence slashed the scrolls to pieces and threw them on the fire. Then he sent an order for the arrest of the prophet and his scribe.

'The King commanded Jerahmeal, a son of the King, Seraiah son of Azriel and Shelemiah son of Abdeel to arrest Baruch the Scribe and Jeremiah the prophet. But the Lord had hidden them' (Jer 36:26).

The names on the bullae are Jerahmeel the King's son, Seraiahu and Berachiah (longer form of Baruch) son of the Scribe. A piece of biblical narrative, photographed in stone![2]

Professor Shiloh died in January 1988. What happened that week revealed the passions that archaeology arouses. Large posters mysteriously appeared in the orthodox quarters celebrating his death. Maimonodes, a medieval Jewish philosopher, was quoted to the effect that even the relatives of a dead heretic should rejoice, wear white, eat, drink and celebrate 'In praise and thanksgiving to the Almighty we inform the public that the wicked heretic and defiler who destroyed Jewish graves on the slope of the Temple Mount, Yigal Shiloh—may his name be blotted out—has died.' The posters went on to recall his suffering during a long illness, and speculated on how much more he would now be suffering in hell.

Next day full-page adverts appeared in the *Jerusalem Post* deploring this example of bad taste and religious vindictiveness, and praising the memory of 'a patriot, a scientist and a true son of Israel.'

Under the Temple Shadow

Equally controversial was the crown and climax of Israeli archaeology—the excavation at the Temple Mount. The very mention of Professor Meir Ben-Dov can ruin a mayor's cocktail-party or a scientific seminar. This maverick figure has fought running battles with Jewish religionists, Arab politicians, United Nations officials, and, for good measure, most of his fellow archaeologists. Breaking all of the accepted rules and introducing techniques that scandalise the scientific establishment, Ben-Dov laboured for twelve years, and created several Guinness-type records.[3]

This excavation was to be *at* the Temple Mount, not *of* it. The golden-domed Muslim shrine with its surrounding plazas is of course *verboten*, but the Temple of Solomon (and its successor in Jesus' day) was more than the modest-sized Holy Place. Around it was a vast complex of porticos, courts, esplanades, staircases, ritual baths and ancillary buildings—almost one and a half million square feet. Some of it was on the flattened summit, and some of it outside the colossal retaining walls 165 feet high, of which the Kotel (the Western or 'Wailing' Wall) is a partial survivor.

The announcement of a projected 'dig' caused immediate reaction. The Sephardic Chief Rabbi feared that it might reveal that the Kotel was not the western wall of the Temple after all, and (with a certain lack of logic) claimed the entire area as 'holy ground'. The Ashkenazi Chief Rabbi added fuel to the fire. What if the Ark of the Covenant were to be found? Since modern Jews are far from being uniformly ceremonially 'clean' and legally 'pure', it would be best to avoid any danger of pollution by putting off any excavation until the Messiah came and superintended them himself.

Ben-Dov was not a patient man. He organised a neat hoodwink by creating a decoy dig in one area, and whilst furious debate and resistance raged there, quietly began the real job unnoticed in a different patch. Presented with a *fait accompli*, the religious had second thoughts, and even engaged him to expose a certain area that aroused their special interest. They were very anxious to cut along the line of the Wall and maybe get some clues to the exact location of the Holy Place.

That drove the Muslims mad. They feared that discoveries would somehow strengthen Jewish claims on the area. Some even seriously believed that the real purpose was to burrow under the Dome of the Rock and cause its collapse. They took the matter to the United Nations who obligingly passed a resolution condemning Israel, with annual persistence. Several Arab nations spoke darkly of a *jehad* (holy war). At this point I had the fairly rare privilege of a conducted tour of the Rabbi's Tunnel, as it was called, not at right-angles to the wall under the Dome, but simply continuing the line of the Wall and on the outside. That was dramatic enough: great grey ashlars from Solomon's original construction, and the openings of channels for blood to be sluiced away from the sacrifices, both topographical clues, too complex for my understanding, which confirmed that the Temple had indeed stood *north* of the Dome, not on its site. There was also a tiny synagogue hewn out of the subterranean rubble, barely large enough to hold the required ten worshippers, directly opposite the calculated site of the Holy of Holies. I crept out, awed.

Repeated UNO and UNESCO opposition came to a head and then collapsed, when the director-general of UNESCO sent a personal representative to the dig. He reported that Arab fears were groundless. At about the same time, significant Muslim areas were reached by the spade—and meticulously preserved. A great Omayyad palace from the seventh century was revealed. Muslims long assumed the mound to be the remains of a Byzantine Christian ruin, but here was evidence of an Arab day of glory. Smiles all round.

But not for long. By now, Ben-Dov's unorthodox methods were scandalising the scholarly world. An archaeologist's normal tools are a small trowel and a camelhair brush, but Ben-Dov brought in a bulldozer. He had his eye on a very large area. His method was to excavate on two planes at once. Horizontally, he cut great swathes with a bulldozer, whilst vertically he sank shafts to anticipate the strata that the machine would expose. 'If the bulldozer operator is graced with a sensitive soul, and if an archaeologist is stationed permanently beside the scoop, it can be a very helpful instrument,' he explained blandly.[4]

Academic colleagues had apoplexy. With demonic energy the dig continued—for twelve years, round-the-clock. (A normal dig would be two or three years, for two months per year.) But Ben-Dov was in the big-time, searching for Israel's soul. Director Benjamin Mazar, venerable father-figure of the archaeological community, fell out with his colourful field-director, and the two began a war of words, each seizing whatever records and results he could lay hands on. Mazar produced a hastily-written popular account of the unfinished dig called *Mountain of the Lord*, but then virtually disowned it, blamed co-writers who had popularised its style, and forbade any review of the book.[5] A full ten years later Ben-Dov came to press with his *In the Shadow of the Temple*.[6] This aroused academic fury. Colleagues stayed away from its publication reception and treated the author as an outcast. Nevertheless, it makes wonderful reading. He has a flair for the evocative and the dramatic that matches Yigael Yadin's. The reader feels the drudgery, the suspense, the moments of discovery, the elation of uncovering a nation's soul. Each chapter is preceded by a colourful setting of the historical scene. Take an example of his style:

> The Patriarch of the Ethiopian Church happened to visit the dig soon after we had uncovered these steps. "Is it possible that Jesus and the Apostles walked up these stairs?" he asked.
> "There's no doubt about it," I told him. "This is the main staircase that led to the Temple."
> Upon hearing my answer, a wave of emotion swept over the Patriarch and his retinue, and we paused so that they could offer up prayer on the spot.

The steps in question were the most dramatic find. Described by Josephus, their discovery was a solemn moment. Two hundred feet long, the great white stairs provided the normal entry to the Temple. Alternate steps are twelve inches and thirty-five inches high, to prevent casual hasty mounting of the stairway, which led to single, double and triple gates described jointly as the Hulda Gates. These opened into upward-sloping subways that in turn broke through the floor of the temple courts. Josephus describes the brightly-coloured decorations that may have provided the nickname of 'Gate Beautiful' (where Peter and John healed the cripple in Jesus' name, preached to the excited crowd that gathered, and were arrested by the temple police: Acts 3 and 4). Fallen blocks and segments of arch bear witness to his accuracy; flowers, fruited vines, geometrical designs, and faint signs of the original vivid colours.

Where Jesus stood

I have a picture of myself standing on the staircase, Bible in hand, ready to introduce a slide sequence on the meaning of all this to the Christian. For not only must Jesus have walked up these steps to worship; my belief is that he stood on them to preach. Another name for the steps was the Rabbis' Staircase.

Here the religious teachers—the Pharisees—often stood haranguing and instructing the slow-moving crocodiles of people who might take five hours to shuffle into the courts above. The Pharisees, remember, were laymen who taught and applied Scripture; the Sadducees were the clergy who officiated at the sacrifices. Pharisees (in spite of Jesus' stricture on some of them) were considerably more spiritually-minded than the worldly, corrupt and compromising priesthood. Suspicious of Herod's motives in rebuilding the Temple, they preferred to teach on the outside steps, or on the only remaining area above not rebuilt by Herod— Solomon's Portico. There, too, Jesus sometimes preached, especially in the cold wet winter when it offered some shelter (Jn 10:22–23). The first apostles did the same (Acts 3:11) and indeed the area became a regular meeting place for the early church, which presumably supplemented the temple worship with its own celebrations, instruction and healing ministry here (Acts 5:12).

But on that final solemn day of Holy Week, when Jesus uttered his last warnings and departed for the Mount of Olives, it was surely on these steps that he stood. Often I've rehearsed his words as I stood there, and marvelled how the whole layout illustrates and underlines his words. Look at Matthew 23. The teachers are at work on the Staircase. 'Then Jesus said to the crowds and to His disciples, "the preachers of the law and the Pharisees sit in Moses' seat"' (verses 1 & 2).

Its popular name is the Rabbi's Steps. 'They love to be greeted in the market places and to have men call them *Rabbi*. But you are not to call them *Rabbi*, for you have only one Master and you are all brothers' (verses 7 & 8). The scene was just outside the great arched doorways: 'You shut the Kingdom of heaven in men's faces. You yourselves do not enter in, nor will you let those enter who are trying to' (verse 14).

Just below are thirty *mikvahs*—ritual baths where (amongst others) Gentile converts to the Jewish faith were immersed. 'You travel over land and sea to win a single convert, and when he becomes one you make him twice as much a son of hell as you are' (verse 15).

To the left are the tombs of Kedron's slope, whitewashed and gleaming in the sun: 'You are like whitewashed tombs, which look beautiful on the outside but on the inside are full of dead men's bones' (verse 27).

Just visible are the decorated tombs of several prophets —Haggai, Zechariah and Malachi (maybe more in those days): 'You build tombs for the prophets and decorate the graves of the righteous... testifying against yourselves that you are the descendants of those who murdered the prophets' (verses 29–32).

Then comes the outburst of agonised rejected love: 'O Jerusalem, Jerusalem... how often have I longed to gather your children together as a hen gathers her chicks under her wings, but you were not willing... You shall not see me again until you say, "Blessed is he who comes in the name of the Lord"' (verses 37–39).

And Jesus leaves the Temple—for Olivet, Upper Room, Gethsemane, and the Cross.

A solemn place. I pause and trail my fingers in one of the *mikvah* pools. Here Mary would have come for her purification after the holy child was born. Here, presumably, the three thousand were baptized on the Day of Pentecost (no problem, as those who doubt immersion used to claim— two hundred baptisteries were surely enough).

Round the corner, the shops of the money-changers have been found—little square booths tucked under the royal staircase whose line can be traced. The priestly families controlled them, and charged exhorbitant sums for foreign currencies to be changed into shekels. Only in shekels could the sacrificial animals be bought. Then came the second racket. You could, in theory, buy your animal anywhere, but a priest had to check it to ensure that it was 'without blemish' and if you hadn't bought it from one of his cousins, then invariably he would find a blemish! 'But don't worry —my cousin over there has animals. I can guarantee *them*.' At anywhere between four and ten times the market price! It was a scandal everyone knew about, but no one could prevent. Popular sayings, now disinterred express the common view. The family of Annas, says one, make their sons priests, their sons-in-law treasurers and their servants beaters of the people. The temple itself was referred to by many Jews as 'the bazaar of Annas.'

No wonder Jesus *twice* attempted to 'cleanse' the temple courts (Jn 2:12–17 and Mat 21:12–13). Some scholars think that unlikely. Why? We have records of attempts by *five* different reformers between the years 30 and 65.

Two stone inscriptions found in the huge dig bear particularly poignant witness to the Temple's fate. The first is on a small pillar into which is cut the name of Titus, the destroying general, and the logo of his famous Tenth Legion. It was found by Ben-Dov's diggers on the ninth day of the month Av. This is observed by world Jewry as a day of fasting and mourning, for both Titus' destruction in 70 AD and Nebuchadnezzar's in 586 BC were completed on that day. The second inscription has not been moved to some museum. It stands where it was found: the carving of a Byzantine cross in the wall beside the steps on which Jesus stood to cry 'O Jerusalem'.

A Roman general brings the judgement of the God of the Jews, to the City of the King, the rabbis themselves acknowledge that. A Roman cross bears on its outspread arms the King of the Jews, whose reign will spread to all nations, even the most hardened sceptic must agree. Judgement experienced—or borne by Another. There are still only the two alternatives, for Jew and Gentile alike.

Notes

1. D J Wiseman, 'Siloam', *The New Bible Dictionary* (Inter Varsity Press 1961), p 1187.
2. 'The Quest for the City of David', *Eretz* Magazine, Autumn 1985, pp 8–22.
3. For a racy account, see Hershal Shanks, 'Excavating in the Shadow of the Temple Mount', *Biblical Archaeological Review* November-December 1986, pp 21–38.
4. Meir Ben-Dov, *In the Shadow of the Temple* (Harper and Row: New York, 1985), p 26.
5. Benjamin Mazor, *Mountain of the Lord* (Doubleday: New York, 1975), with Gaalyah Cornfeld and David Noel Freedman.
6. See note 4.

Part Three

The Teacher

About that time there lived Jesus, a wise man,
if indeed one ought to call him a man.
For he was one who wrought surprising feats
and was a teacher of such people as accept
the truth gladly....
And the tribe of the Christians so called after him,
has still to this day not disappeared.

(Flavius Josephus—around 90 AD)

Jesus! the name that charms our fears,
That bids our sorrows cease;
'Tis music in the sinner's ears,
'Tis life, and health, and peace.

(Charles Wesley—around 1745)

8

The Beloved Lake

Doctor Jim Fleming is a fascinating person to talk to. An American Christian, he gained his PhD by perfecting audio-visual aids to the historic-geographical study of the land of Israel, and is a mine of information on the culture and customs of first-century Galilee. One day we were standing by the Sea of Galilee. 'Don't imagine that the fishermen-disciples of Jesus were poor unskilled men. Galilee fishing was a vital part of the economy of the Middle East. About a thousand boats were engaged on this small stretch of water,' the Doctor said, gesturing toward the Lake.

I slipped in a piece of just-acquired knowledge of which I was rather proud. 'I've just read that Strabo, the Roman historian, describes the fish from Migdal as very popular in the markets of Rome. Would that be Magdala?'

'That's right. Mary Magdalene, as we call her, was Mary from Migdal, a few miles south of Capernaum. The main fishing centres were Migdal Noonia (Tower of the Fish), Capernaum (Village of Nahum) and Bethsaida (Fish-town). In fact there may have been at least three Bethsaidas! Huge quantities of fresh-water fish still come down from the Upper Jordan into the northern end of the Lake.'

'I'm told that you have come across some old fishermen's tales from the time of Jesus,' I prompted him.

He laughed. 'Yes—the priestly families were particularly keen on fish. One man boasted that he could sit down his guests to a meal of two hundred different kinds of fish. Another challenges his friends to test his palate. Catch a fish anywhere in the land, he says: cook it and serve it to me. After one mouthful I shall tell you what kind of fish it is. After two mouthfuls, I shall tell you where you caught it. Apparently in those days, the tall tales were told by the men who ate the fish, not those who caught them!'

I pressed this fascinating man a little further. 'Can we make any informed guesses about the fishermen Jesus called to be his disciples?'

'Well yes. Notice that the brothers Peter and Andrew worked with Zebedee and his two sons James and John—plus several hired men and more than one boat (Mk 1:16–20). That implies quite a large scale business. Now here's another possible clue. When Jesus was arrested and taken to the high-priest's house, Peter and John were able to get into the premises because they knew the family (Jn 18:15). That *could* imply that "Zebedee, Sons and Partners, Galilee Fish a Specialty," held the monopoly or providing fish for the high-priest's household.'

We strolled along the shore near Capernaum; sometimes easy walking, and sometimes hard scrambling over black basalt boulders. Jim pointed to a horseshoe bay about two hundred yards across. 'Remember how Jesus sat in Peter's boat and preached to the crowd gathered around the shore? That's almost certainly the place. As you see, the land forms a natural amphitheatre. It has been proved possible to talk to at least ten thousand people here without the aid of amplifying equipment.'

I shielded my eyes from the sun and peered towards the summit of the rising ground. 'Surely that's the traditional site of the Sermon on the Mount?'

'Yes, the sound works both ways. People sitting or standing all over the slopes would be able to hear Jesus speaking from the top.'

Called to catch others

We stood and watched modern-day Galilee fishermen trawling off-shore from boats whose general size and shape have not greatly altered since New Testament times. There is no difficulty in saying to yourself 'Jesus stood here.'

Few modern buildings obstruct; in fact the area is less built-up now than it was in his day. I recalled with glee the Sunday-school class back in England, whose teacher was relating the incident of the great catch of fish recorded in Luke 5. Having told how Peter, reluctant at first, eventually followed Jesus' bidding and dropped the nets where instinct and experience would tell him there were no prospects, the teacher added, 'What do you think Peter said to Jesus when he found the nets full of fish?' Quick as a flash came back the reply from one cockney lad, who has doubtless gone far by now in street-trading: 'Same time, same place, termorrer!'

In fact Peter said something quite different: in effect, 'Get out of my life.' It was a traumatic moment. A carpenter had just told a fisherman where to catch fish. He was already known to Peter as a rabbi, and more. There was a tussle going on for lordship in Peter's life here; what F B Meyer called 'the settlement as to supreme authority.' A disturbing thought had occurred—'If this teacher can see to the depths of the lake perhaps he can see to the depths of my heart. I'm not sure I like that.' So—when Peter saw such a large number of fish, he fell at Jesus knees and said, 'Go away from me Lord; I am a sinful man' (Lk 5:8). But Jesus said, 'Don't be afraid; from now on you will catch men.' So they pulled their boats up on shore, left everything and followed him (Lk 5:11).

Is it too much to say that in that incident are found all the principles at work in any man or woman's sense of calling to trust Christ for personal salvation and to follow Christ in public service? An awed sense is awakened that in the figure of Jesus I have met someone very human and yet bigger than any human category; an uncomfortable awareness of my own soiled past and sinful inclinations; a heart tugged two ways at once, away from him and towards him; an inward struggle as to who is really going to run my life, and how many areas of it are going to have to come under his sway—and a conviction, the moment that issue is settled, that if he can do something with even *my* life, then he can do it for anyone and everyone, and that I must take every opportunity to tell them so: 'Follow me—catch men.'

Incidentally, many of the details in these fishing stories are so authentic that we are obviously reading eye-witness accounts and personal memories. It is simply silly to say, as so many modern 'scholars' airily suggest, that these are pious myths that have gradually arisen to give expression to spiritual truths. Either these things happened, or the Gospel writers are very clever and deliberate liars: there is no middle choice. Even the different types of fishing nets employed in Galilee are distinguished. Peter and Andrew were using casting-nets—*amphiblestron*—attached to 5 ft wooden cross-bars, thrown from the beach and drawn back in with cords (Mat 4:18). James and John were repairing their deep-water drop-nets *diktna*—when Peter called them across to help (Lk 5:5). During the night they would have been trawling with drag-nets—*sagere*—which Jesus later made into a symbol of the kind of evangelism that catches the attention of many different types of people who will later have to be sorted out (Mat 13:47).

Jesus' home town

One of my favourite photographs shows Rita and two strangers, man and wife, standing in an arched doorway

surrounded by blazing red and violet bougainvillaea. Over
the archway, a fading notice announces 'Capernaum—The
Town of Jesus. Open daily, 8.30–16.30'. The wording
always amuses me. I'm so glad that the offer of Christ's
gospel does not close in the mid-afternoon! In fact we talked
to that couple, tourists from England, and our conversation
about Christ perhaps bore fruit (or if ours didn't someone
else's did), for several years later we found them eagerly
serving Christ in a pioneer city-centre situation in England.

Kefar Nahum stands empty and silent when the tourists
have left. But so much has been excavated that one can
walk its echoing stone streets past its ruins now only two
feet high, and easily imagine the bustling metropolis, fishing
harbour, millstone industry and commercial quarter that
was once indeed Jesus' home-town. Here the great Via
Mares (road from the Mediterranean) emerged from the
Jezreel Valley and joined the road to the east as it swung
around the north shore of the lake. Here a major taxation
centre drew in the revenue paid reluctantly to the Romans
for every article that was transported through this
communications junction. One of the tax-officers (Levi
renamed Matthew) became a disciple of Jesus and used his
shorthand skills to record the words of the Master—
Matthew's Gospel. Here the two territories of Herod's rival
sons Antipas and Philippus marched side by side. Here a
Roman garrison lived under its centurians, one of whom
had such respect for the One God of the Jews that he
financed the building of a synagogue, subsequently meeting
Jesus and expressing a humble confidence which delighted
him and brought healing to the officer's personal servant
(Lk 7:1–10).

Where Jesus taught?

The ruins of a beautiful white fourth-century limestone
synagogue just by the fishing quarter are often pointed out

as 'the synagogue of Jesus.' This is a typical piece of tourist shorthand. The building from Jesus' time is actually underneath the structure—a much simpler building of black basalt with a rough cobbled floor, perhaps eighty feet long with a colonnaded community centre and school hall alongside. But only a hundred yards from it is a more startling discovery. Guides, as is their wont, casually toss out the claim that they are pointing to 'St Peter's house' or 'Jesus' home.' The experienced tourist, having been treated to several outrageously pinpointed sites like this, is inclined to say 'Oh yeah?' and walk on. That would be a mistake. It is as likely as anything can be outside the Bible that this is indeed Jesus' home.

In the year 380 AD, Aegeria, a Spanish Christian pilgrim, visited Capernaum. He recorded a remarkable juxtaposition of Jews and Christians living amicably together (sadly rare by that time) the synagogue and the church building almost adjoining. The former, 'white with great steps leading up to it' is clearly the one you can still see. The church, described as eight-sided, has been recently built, says the pilgrim, over the ruin of an older house church, in such a way as to preserve what remains of its walls. That house church in turn had been an enlargement of what the narrator calls 'the house of the prince of the apostles' (ie Peter).

And there it all is, uncovered by the spades of modern archaeology. An octagonal building is in places oddly arched over the remains of older walls which in turn show signs of an earlier building. Mark's Gospel refers no less than eleven times to the house of Peter's mother-in-law, who was healed of a fever by Jesus immediately after his first appearance in the synagogue. This seems to have become Jesus' home and a kind of Bible-seminary for the first disciples. It was the normal way for a rabbi to work; gathering between eight and fifteen disciples who (either all together or taking it in turns) lived with him, attended to his simple needs, listened to his table-talk, watched how he handled people, and privately questioned him about his public teaching.

The old original floor was found by the excavators to be strewn with plaster fallen in from the walls. Over a hundred pieces had graffiti written on them, including references to Peter, prayers to Jesus, and descriptions of him as the Messiah, the Most High, the Good and the Lord.

So, the clues fit, the guides are not pulling our legs, and we are very probably looking at Jesus' adopted home. Imagine the scene, then. The houses in this quarter are *insulae*: extended households with as many as fifteen rooms (as the family grows by birth or marriage, you simply add more rooms). Houses were not so much to *live* in, as to sleep in and store possessions in. Sometimes the house is quiet as the Master gives private teaching to his little band of disciples (as when he explains to them the real meaning of the parable of the sower in Matthew 13:2–10). Sometimes the courtyard is packed with a casually assembled congregation, overflowing into all of the rooms, which are interconnected by open windows.

Once four men desperate to help their paralysed friend, break through the simple roof (replacable every winter) and lower him at Jesus' feet (Luke 5:18–19). One unforgettable evening, at least, the adjoining streets are crowded with an excited mob of the sick, the curious, the troublemakers, the enquirers: 'the whole town was gathered at the door' (Mk 1:32–34).

That immediately followed a startling day when Jesus had exorcised a demon-possessed man within the synagogue, then returned to the nearby house and healed Peter's mother-in-law. Again all of these accounts bear the stamp of eye-witness memories, not of legends that grew long afterwards. The scene is right, the customs are correct, the atmosphere is authentic. Jesus was here: he said these things and performed these deeds. Quite shortly afterwards, Jews and Gentiles alike who wished it had never happened, tried to account for it all in different ways, calling Jesus a magician or worse. It never seems to have occurred to them to deny that it all actually happened. They knew better.

Still Christ calls

Back in England, preaching in a Suffolk village chapel, I tried my best to picture the scene. 'You may say—that is all very moving and persuasive, but what can it mean to us? We shall never see Capernaum. We cannot spend three years with Jesus, listening to his table talk and watching the way he handles people.'

Several people looked up at me, quite obviously thinking exactly that. I went on, 'But you needn't say that. For the very presence of the Holy Spirit means that Jesus will become all to you that he was to his first disciples. You cannot live with him? But he offers to live with you! "If anyone hears my voice and opens the door, I will go in and eat with him and he with me"' (Rev 3:20).

'You cannot listen to his teaching you say? But you can: it is all recorded by those who first heard it. Read the Gospel narratives, part of God's inspired Word. "Ah, but I cannot question him privately about its meaning," you say. But you can do that, too. Make a daily appointment with him: read the Bible, and pray that he will explain its meaning to you. Millions do it every day.

And what about that wonderful experience of watching how he handles people? That is exactly what you begin to do when you really come into the fellowship of the church.

Don't just "go to church" but give time and trouble to the gathering of God's believing people, worshipping with them, sharing your discoveries, praying for each other, listening to each other's experiences. All over the place, churches are waking up to what this means. Get into it and discover it for yourself.'

We had a moment of silent prayer in the little chapel, and then three people raised their hands to show that they wanted to know the living Christ. One said to me next time I met him, 'I listened fascinated, and thought—*"This is real, but it can't be for me."* Then, when you prayed, my heart began to thump, and I started to sweat, and I thought, *"Either I'm having a heart-attack, or I'm getting converted."* Well —I got converted!'

Jesus still calls us,

....o'er the tumult
of the world's wild restless sea,
Day by day His sweet voice soundeth,
Saying, Christian, follow Me.

As of old, apostles heard it,
By the Galilean lake
Turned from home and toil and kindred
Leaving all for His dear sake.[1]

Twentieth century disciples

A group of Jewish young adults asked to talk to me, a few miles out of Capernaum. Someone had pointed me out, as I paddled barefoot along the seashore, as 'that preacher from Jerusalem.' They told me of their faith in Jesus, and the high price they had to pay for it. Most Israelies have an attitude of live-and-let-live, but not the ultra-orthodox. These very earnest and vociferous enthusiasts are in direct line from the Pharisees of Jesus' day, and I've heard more than one secular Israeli refer to them irritably as Pharisees. Some of them had employed a species of religious Scargillism to prevent the Messianic Believers of Galilee from worshipping. A hundred had turned up one Sabbath morning, jeering and threatening the worshippers in their little hall. Next week it was five hundred, and the next a thousand. They promised five thousand the following Sabbath. At that point the local Mayor, himself one of the *Hassidim*, said correctly, that he had a near-riot situation. So he closed the meeting-hall that he said, incorrectly, was the cause of the trouble.

Since then the followers of Jesus have 'gone underground' meeting somewhere different each week, by prior arrangement. Yet such is the attractiveness of their faith, and such is the reality of the presence of Jesus amongst them, that Jews, Arabs and Gentiles attach themselves to their little group and in turn put their faith in the Saviour.

There is a lovely Scottish Hospice at Tiberius, Herod's Galilee capital apparently never visited by Jesus. The Church of Scotland has a chapel there, and the hospice (ie pilgrim's guest house) is a series of black stone buildings just back from the shore. Originally a hospital, it stands in fine grounds full of the whole blaze and glory of Galilee trees, shrubs and flowers. Josephus wrote lyrically of the local vegetation:

> Thanks to the rich soil, there is not a plant that does not flourish; the air is so temperate that it suits the most diverse varieties. The winter-loving walnut grows luxuriantly beside the palm which thrives on heat, and side by side with the fig and the olive. One might deem it nature's crowning ambition to place together in a single spot the most discordant species in healthy rivalry.[2]

The Talmud, with pardonable exaggeration, assures us that fruit grew as rapidly as the deer runs, and the fruit is so light and sweet that a man can eat a hundred pieces and not feel full.

To the Jewish sages, in fact, Galilee was the Beloved Lake. When God made the seven seas, they tell us, he pronounced them good. But when he made Galilee, he found his delight. To that, every Christian will say a hearty *amen*, for here we have found *our* delight too—the One of whom the Father bore witness in the words 'This is my beloved Son, in whom is all my delight' (Lk 3:22).

The Church of Scotland does not attempt mission work amongst Jews or Arabs seeing itself rather as a provision for expatriate Christians. Nevertheless, the efficiency of their establishment, the sense of vocation expressed by the staff, and the preaching heard at the chapel, bear gentle witness to Jesus. I heard, from a burly Scottish minister by the name of Craig, one of the finest expositions I have ever heard of what the Puritans used to call 'The Glorious Exchange' the apostle's great words, 'God made him (Jesus) who had no sin to be sin for us, so that in him we might become the righteousness of God' (2 Cor 5:21).

Nearby, Avner Ram, one of Israel's finest professional guides with an encyclopaedic knowledge of the Bible, showed me the hot springs of Tiberius. They are back in use, offering treatment for skin disorders and rheumatic illnesses. Their presence accounted for Herod's decision to build one of his many palaces there (with a gold roof, it was said). It also explains what often puzzled me as a child hearing the Bible stories. Why did everyone around Galilee seem to be *sick*? Now I know. Because Galilee was where the sick went: the Bath or the Harrogate, or one might also say the Lourdes, of the ancient Middle East.

One tradition stated that if a leper knelt all night in one of the streams, fell asleep and dreamed, then he would awaken cured. As in the New Testament, 'leprosy' was a rather imprecise word meaning any disfiguring skin disease, and was not used exclusively to describe the appalling disease for which a cure has only recently been found.

Interestingly, the two men whom Jesus healed in quick succession at Capernaum represented the two ailments which most regularly drove sufferers to Galilee (Luke 5:12–19). Sandwiched between the call of four disciples to leave their fishing and the call of another to leave his tax-collecting, the whole string of stories bear unintended and coincidental witness to the total accuracy of Luke's account of the way of life prevalent around Capernaum.

The boat that came back

From 1984 to 1986 there were drought conditions in Galilee, and the level of the lake dropped severely. Two Israeli brothers from a nearby Kibbutz were hopefully exploring the enlarged shore when they found forty ancient coins scattered in the mud. Digging around for more, they came across fragments of wood and the obvious outline of a boat. Events moved rapidly, with that mixture of zany humour, religious excitement, eye for the main chance and glorious exaggeration which are typical ingredients of life in modern Israel.

The brothers dutifully reported their find to the authorities, who tried to keep the lid on it, since digging holes and finding things is a very popular hobby. Unfortunately someone 'leaked' and hordes of hopefuls with spades began to scour the shore. Decoy holes were hurriedly dug and then half covered so as to midlead people. The television people turned up. Rumour had it that 'the boat of Jesus' had been discovered. The Minister of Tourism, quick to see the possibilities announced a 'major Christian relic' and started taking out tenders for the building of a 'shrine'!

Ultra-orthodox Jews organised more demonstrations, claiming that the whole thing was a con-trick organised by missionaries, (the worst thing they can call anyone). A party of Christian Eskimos arrived from Alaska, clamouring to see it.

As the drought ended and the water rose, a race against time developed to prize the wreck loose, lift it clear without destroying it, and then preserve it, bearing in mind the delicacy of the wood which was eighty per cent waterlogged. The kind of skills employed on the Tudor *Mary Rose* in England were invoked, and the water-content of the wood was gradually replaced with polyethylene glycol, which eventually solidifies.

Of course the craft does fall short of being Jesus' boat (or even Peter's boat) but it is an unique example of the kind of little ship that appears in the Gospels. The age is roughly right. The boat is thirty feet long, rather tubby (seven feet wide) and distinctly shallow (four feet deep). It reminds me, in shape and size, of a Yorkshire 'cobble'. The planks are held together by mortice-and-tennon joints (simply— pegs in one plank, holes in the next). It was part-decked and propelled by one sail and three or four pairs of oars. Most strikingly, it closely resembles a Christian mosaic of a boat from the earliest centuries, already found outside nearby Migdal. A few objects were still inside the ruined craft: arrowheads, net-weights, a cooking pot, an oil-lamp.

Meeting Christ on the beach

Not long before the boat was found, a group of us stood on the shore north of Migdal and just short of Capernaum. By ancient tradition, the little shingle beach is the place where Jesus met his fishermen-disciples after his death and resurrection (Jn 21). It could well be so.

Half of the events we associate with his ministry happened in an amazingly small area. You can row a mile offshore and take one photograph which will encompass most of it.

At some time in the past, pious folk have laid six great flat heart-shaped stones across the tiny beach and into the water. They represent, one assumes, the thrice-repeated question of Jesus to Peter, 'Lovest thou me?' (Jn 21:15–17) and the three replies. Thirty of us stood on the fine shingle, as little ripples plashed and played over the stones. A fishing boat was anchored a hundred yards off-shore; just the correct distance to illustrate the story. I read the matchless tale and commented on it.

Clearly the whole incident was carefully stage-managed by Jesus. Every detail was set up to stir memories and awaken consciences. Every scene in the act was a replay of previous occasions. An unrecognised stranger shows men

who have fished unsuccessfully all night where to catch
fish—and the nets are filled: a replay of that unforgettable
scene when he first called them. Bread and fish await them
by a lake as Jesus distributes the food: a replay of the
feeding of the five thousand. A *charcoal* fire (anthracion)
burns; the word is only used once elsewhere: 'It was cold,
and the servants and officials stood around an *anthracion*
they had made to keep warm. Peter was standing with
them, warming himself....' (Jn 18:18).

He warmed himself at the world's fire, and was soon
denying his Lord (as we invariably do, if that's the warmth
we seek). Now Jesus invites Peter to warm himself at *his* fire,
and pick up the task of discipleship once more.

And, of course, I read the famous three questions.

'Peter, do you *love* me more than these', (with *agape*—
deep unshaken, divine love).

'Well Lord, you know that I'm very fond of you' (*philia*).

'Peter—do you truly *love* me?'

'Well Lord, we are *friends*—I dare to say that.'

'Alright Peter—let's start when you can honestly start.
Are we *friends*, then?'

'Master, you know my heart, you know we are.'

'Then from that modest beginning, I can fan the flames
of friendship into deep, divine, love, so that you give a
lifetime to tending my sheep and feeding my lambs—and
then go willingly to a martyr's death.'

So we might paraphrase the moving exchange.

I paused on the question that Bible-readers sometimes
discuss.

'Do you truly love me *more than these*?' asked Jesus. More
than who? Or what? Perhaps 'more than these fish' since
the bewildered disciples, not knowing what else to do after
those traumatic events, had surely taken a backward step in
returning to their fishing.

Or perhaps 'more than these other disciples' since only a
few days ago Peter had insisted that even if all the others

abandoned Jesus, *he* wouldn't—and with what a pathetic follow-through.

Douglas was one of our party, a big man, owner of a business in England. Owner, too, of a splendid camera, with which he had come to Israel with the intention of taking first-class pictures. Until the security men at the airport examined it—and accidentally broke it! Douglas had tried everywhere to get it repaired. Not a chance. For several days he was really angry and frustrated as a succession of breathtaking views and marvellous sunsets mocked his inability to capture any of them on film. Now as I finished my little homily, he approached me trembling with emotion.

'Do you love me *more than these*' he quoted. 'It has just dawned on me that I've been missing the whole point of the trip to Israel. This isn't a place to take nice pictures; it's the place where Christ walked. Do you know Don, as you read that story, it seemed to me Jesus was saying to me, "Douglas, do you love me *more than these photographs*?" Well—I want to get this clear once and for all. Who's running my life? Would you baptise me?'

I was glad to. This was no spur-of-the-moment decision and I knew it. Next day we baptised Douglas in the river Jordan, where it flows out of the lake, together with his daughter Ruth. We also baptised Stan and Anne, who had felt the touch of the living Christ at the Garden Tomb three days earlier, and Doris, a pensioner, who, back in Essex, had tried to tell people at the Women's Meeting that she didn't know whether she was a Christian or not. Doris' doubts had been poo-poohed until Rita talked to her and explained that grace which offers salvation and assurance as a free gift, asking only the empty hand outstretched to take it.

Douglas subsequently sold his business, and now works unpaid for the Belgian Evangelical Mission. Ruth took training with Moorlands Bible College and Wycliffe Translators, preparing to take the gospel to Africa. Stan and Anne in their business and Doris in her home-life, have borne shining witness to the reality of Jesus, and attracted others to him.

Jesus calls us from the worship
Of the vain world's golden shore,
From each idol that would keep us,
Saying, "Christian love Me more?"[3]

Notes

1. Hymn, 'Jesus calls us o'er the tumult' Cecil Frances Alexander, 1818–95.
2. Josephus, *The Wars of the Jews*, Book 3: Chapter 10 para 8, p 250.
3. See Note 1 above.

9

Not Like the Scribes

Susan Marcos is undoubtedly one of Israel's best professional guides. Jewish-American by background, she and her family have paid a high price for making *allyah* back to Israel. All of them need to work long hard hours to make ends meet. One son has lost a leg in the Israeli Defence Force. One of her poems asks,

> To what have we come?
> This land, desolate, neglected:
> Tears of sand fill dry riverbeds.
> Suddenly a bloom, a blade of grass
> Quickens the heart of the soil
> Already soaked with the blood of centuries.
>
> Was it always thus?
> Trails of awesome pen and power
> Boom and roll over the same roads our ancestors walked.

Susan and I have walked together over those 'same roads' following the footprints of Jesus. Our alliance was a simple arrangement. At each place where Jesus had spoken and acted, she would sketch, for our tourists, the background of custom, culture and religion. Then I gave the implica

tions. For example, she described a house with its low walls
and tiled or turfed roof, and showed how easily a paralysed
man could be lowered through the roof at Jesus' feet (Mk
2:1–5). Then I expounded the impact of Jesus' amazing
words to the cripple, 'Your sins are forgiven. Rise up and
walk.'

As Susan smilingly, noncommital, said on one such occasion, 'There's the humanity of Jesus—now over to Don for
the deity!'

As we walked along a ruler-straight road in the Jezreel
valley, the surrounding fields thick with produce (for he
who claimed to be the Bread of Life hailed from the vale
known as the bread-basket of Israel), Susan explained how
an itinerant rabbi lived and worked. With his dozen or so
disciples he tramped from village to village, carrying his
sheepskin diploma of rabbinical training. The inevitable
small boys would dash ahead to their villages to announce
his coming. The people would pour out to meet him, still
well outside the village, and the 'preaching' would begin
immediately as the excited noisy procession covered the
last mile. Not for nothing is Luke's Gospel patterned as a
seemingly endless walking-tour which gives the major part
of that account its literary shape.

At first sight Jesus must have resembled a typical travel-
ling rabbi, except that he had no sheepskin diploma, as was
scornfully pointed out—'The Jews were amazed and asked,
"How did this man get such learning without having
studied?"' (Jn 7:15).

But the more he talked, the more it became evident that
this was no ordinary rabbi. Susan's emphasis on 'humanity'
and mine on 'deity' become bewilderingly intertwined.
'When Jesus had finished saying these things, the crowds
were amazed at his teaching, because he taught as one who
had authority, and not as their teachers of the law' (Mat
7:28–29). What did they mean? Surely it was supposed to
be the official teachers who had the authority and Jesus

who was unauthorised?

They were referring to his style. The job of the scribes was to hunt down matters of fact and precedent in the huge collection of written and oral tradition, often to settle some social or legal dispute. The Pharisees went further and tried to interpret and apply the material to moral and religious issues.

Their method was to quote some Bible incident, then invoke a number of varying interpretations of it—what rabbi so-and-so said about it three hundred years ago—what (on the other hand) my rabbi thought it meant when I asked him ten years ago—what a recent court-case decided on the point—what a line in one of the psalms says that may possibly have some bearing on it—and by the way, I heard a story the other day—and so on, almost *ad infinitum*. Much of this was purely oral in Jesus' time, and referred to as the tradition of the elders. Within another four hundred years (with all the further additions and comments of those centuries) it became at last encapsulated in the Talmud—a collection of mind-numbing complexity which you can take a life-time to find your way around. I've often lingered outside the window of a *yeshiva* (study-school) and watched the awesome spectacle of young men and old spending literally that lifetime simply raising hypothetical questions, scurrying from one scroll to another to find precedents, chanting quotations, and loudly taking up opposing positions.

Jesus dismissed some of this (not all) in terse words. 'Some Pharisees and teachers of the law asked Jesus, "Why do your disciples break the tradition of the elders? They don't wash their hands before they eat"' (Mat 15:1). (This was not a matter of hygiene, but of scrupulously following a developed ritual of ceremonial washing and blessings.)

Jesus replied, 'And why do *you* break the command of *God* for the sake of your *tradition*? ... You nullify the word of God for the sake of your tradition!' He goes on to take two typical examples of the process in which a welter of comments and customs simply obscure the plain meaning of God's commands (Mat 15:1–12).

The *authority* which Jesus displayed, therefore, was his manner of cutting through human traditions to the plain meaning of God's word—or shining dazzling new light on its implications. And the simple stark formula that went with it? *I say unto you.* That is authority! The certainty of someone with words from God.

Sunshine in Nazareth

My pulpit one Sunday was a carpenter's bench. What could be more appropriate on a Nazareth hilltop in the chapel of a Christian hospital? Visible behind my shoulder as I preached was a panoramic view of Jesus' home town, and in the far distance the mountain village of Nain. Jesus interrupted the funeral of a widow's son up there. In the very same area Elisha, eight centuries earlier, had done the same for another widow's son (Lk 7:11–17 & 2 Kings 8). In both cases those who received God's kindness were non-Jews. That fact, underlined by Jesus in this same town of Nazareth, so infuriated his hearers that they tried to lynch him. (Lk 4:24–30). Curious how newcomers to an exclusive club can in turn become passionate defenders of its closed shop! Galileans, in fact, were not racially true Jews at all. A polyglot people of pagan origins, forcibly settled long ago by a dictator to replace the 'lost' tribes of Israel, they had been converted by force to the Jewish faith during the brief halcyon days of Jewish political independence under the Macabbees. Jerusalemites regarded them with amused contempt rather than the hatred that they held for the Samaritans, whose origins were similar, but who had a rival temple (Jn 4:19–24). Today's descendants of the Galileans are (arguably at least) the Palestinians—another odd turn to the wheel of Middle Eastern ironies!

Rita and I bought some lucious fruit in the Nazareth street market at a ludicrously low price, and ate it gratefully in the blazing heat of mid-day, squatting on a flat stone beside the ancient synagogue which stands on the site of Jesus' famous sermon.

The glorious melody of his words ran through our minds as we recalled it. Not his own words, in fact, but a quotation from Isaiah 61.

'The Spirit of the Lord is on me because he has anointed me to preach good news to the poor. He has sent me to proclaim freedom for the prisoners and recovery of sight for the blind, to release the oppressed, to proclaim the year of the Lord's favour' (Is 61:1–2).

The fiftieth year

Rita had become intrigued by the subject of the Year of Jubilee. This astonishing and neglected Old Testament teaching proposes a national slate-wiping exercise at fifty year intervals. Debts are to be cancelled, slaves released, and property returned to those families compelled by poverty to sell it. In one simple stroke, the principal causes of social injustice, class warfare and revolution, were banished at regular intervals.

We made two startling discoveries. The synagogues did in fact have a lectionary—a set of Scripture readings linked with the calendar. Jesus presumably turned to the set reading for that Sabbath in Galilee. But in that calendar, Leviticus 25 is linked with Isaiah 61. And Leviticus 25 is the Jubilee command.[1] The connection is obvious, once you have the clue. Jubilee is all about new beginnings; Isaiah's Messiah offers such a new start; Jesus brings new life. Jubilee rescued the poor from their poverty; Isaiah brings good news to the poor; Jesus promises the Kingdom to the poor in spirit. Jubilee emptied the prisons, Isaiah proclaims freedom for the prisoner, Jesus sets the captive free.

That was our first discovery. The second followed on its heels. It is widely assumed that Israel never seriously attempted the ideal of Jubilee. (Incidentally, what would modern monetarism make of the system? The imagination boggles! I once preached on it in a parish church in the prosperous south-east of England. After explaining the radical terms, I paused and said, 'We'll now have a few moments of respectful silence whilst bank-managers estate-agents and policemen are carried out or helped into the fresh air to recover!' It caused a ripple of rueful mirth.) But it now seems evident that some nominal attempt was made to observe it. Certainly the calculations were kept up and the Jubilee Year marked in some way. And here comes the shock. Assuming that Jesus was born in 4 BC, his public ministry must have begun in the year 26 AD. But 26 AD was due to be the next Year of Jubilee![2]

A synagogue sensation

We gazed at the locked door of the Nazareth synagogue and in imagination pictured the scene behind it. Every Jubilee pointed on to *the* Jubilee (in Jewish minds) when Messiah would bring, not merely a one-year social readjustment, but the New Age.

'Then he rolled up the scroll, gave it back to the attendant and sat down. The eyes of everyone in the synagogue were fastened on him, and he said to them, "Today this scripture is fulfilled in your hearing"' (Lk 4:20–21). No wonder they said 'Who's this?' And no wonder they winced when, having made the stunning claim to be Israel's Messiah, he apparently snatched it back from them with irritating words about *non-Jews* getting the benefits!

We sat in silence. There were so many avenues to explore. Was Jubilee a clue to all that teaching about trust and worry, about physical needs and eyes set on God's Kingdom? After all, identical words are used. 'You may as

'*What will we eat* in the seventh year if we do not plant or harvest our crops?"' (Lev 25:20). A practical enough question, when the fiftieth year inevitably followed a forty-ninth which was a Sabbath-rest for the land left uncultivated for twelve months. The question is echoed—and answered—by Jesus.

'Do not set your heart on *what you will eat* or drink: do not worry about it...seek God's Kingdom, and these things will be given to you as well' (Lk 12:29–31).

Those odd parables about a rich man's steward who cheerfully cancels his employer's credit-notes—and a banker who waives enormous debts—to say the least, they start to fit into a new scenario in 26 AD. Was Jesus saying repeatedly 'God's Jubilee has come—in me. Be ready for the radical life-style to which I call you. Put God's Kingdom first'? It is a point to which every Christian traveller in Israel returns again and again. The *teaching* of Jesus (as distinct from his cross and resurrection) is at the same time a radical call to a single, trustful life-style, *and* an immensely complex labyrinth of Old Testament allusions, prophetic promises with undreamt-of meanings, and towering personal claims. He may never have said in so many words, 'I am God' (the phrase in the Jewish Middle East would be so shocking as to be incomprehensible and without meaning). But in a hundred different ways *by implication*, that is exactly what he was saying. What else when he embraces every Old Testament title of God? Shepherd, judge, king, physician, jubilee, rock, light, bridegroom, vineyard-owner, saviour, foundation, life-giver. Who *is* this?

Theology in Bethlehem

Two of us were scrambling over the olive-studded slopes of the Judaean hills overlooking Galilee. Herod's frowning fortress was below us, on the long slope down towards the Dead Sea. The olive-leaves shimmered in the breeze with rippling waves of pale green and silver.

My companion was a Christian theologian of high repute. He had just tossed out a provocative remark. 'You know, Paul wasn't the first theologian but the second—Jesus was the first.'

Dr Kenneth Bailey has two unusual qualifications. He has worked for five years in a literacy team, living in isolated Arabic villages that have remained virtually unchanged since Jesus' time. He has spent a lifetime pastoring small Christian congregations in similar remote areas of Egypt and Lebanon. His Bible teaching has therefore been aimed at a society and culture almost identical to that of Jesus' day. The attitudes, values, customs, relationships and responses of these Arab congregations are the same as those of Jesus' hearers.

This is where the parables of Jesus come in—and my friend's tossed-off remark. Story telling was (and is) the supreme Oriental truth medium. Although the parables were unique, they were stories. Memorable, poetic, humorous, witty, they were above all shocking. For repeatedly, Bailey has discovered, the characters in the parables do things that defy custom, turn values upside down, and startle the hearers so thoroughly that they will never forget the impact.

One he had the clue, Doctor Bailey went about systematically recording the reactions he got when discussing details of the stories. What would you make of a woman wiping someone's feet with her hair? What would a son mean by asking for his inheritance before his father had died? It became evident that in Jesus' parables people were always doing quite unthinkable things.

Take the story of the man who wakens his neighbour at midnight to ask for three loaves to feed an unexpected guest (Lk 11). It was a perfectly normal request. Within the solidarity of the village, a visitor was the guest of the whole community. Hospitality was a sacred duty. Several houses holds would immediately pool their resources. Jesus is posing a humorous question, 'Can you imagine a man who is asked to help with hospitality refusing, with absurd chatter about it being late, the children in bed and so on?' The amused reply of the listeners would be, 'No, of course not. It's unthinkable.' 'Quite so,' replies Jesus. 'And how much more unthinkable that God should refuse to answer the prayers of his people.

The point of the story is not the persistent asking of the petitioner (he doesn't *have* to ask repeatedly. The parable doesn't say his friend refused at first—it says refusal would be unthinkable). The 'without-shame' referred to in verse 8 (misunderstood by western readers as persistence or shameless begging) is the 'unshamed honour' of the awakened householder who, *for his reputation's sake* cannot and will not refuse. God's glory is at stake in his answering of prayer.

Customs and culture

As we walked, I contributed what little knowledge I could boast. 'The man who declined to follow Jesus until he had buried his father is an example, isn't it? I think most of us even in the west suspect that his father hadn't actually died.'

'No, of course not,' smiled Doctor Bailey. 'To bury your father is a phrase still used today—I've heard it more than once. It means to put off major decisions and changes in lifestyle until you have become the heir and the head of the family—maybe in ten, fifteen years time. Incidentally, the similar story that goes with that one—the young man who asks permission to run home and say goodbye to his family before he joined the disciples—that one really *is* a shocker. To say goodbye or beg leave, means to call a family conference and have a lengthy discussion, after which the family gives permission for you to leave home. Jesus brushed all

that aside and said, "Make up your own mind, come now."
I've actually seen Lebanese students go white-faced with
shock as I told the story. It implies the claim of Jesus to
over-ride the most rigid family rights. Only God can make
such a claim.'

He warmed to his theme, as we ate pitta bread, cheese
and dates, in the shade of a eucalyptus tree.

'You see, the truths that come repeatedly in the episodes
and the parables are always very much the same. The
absolute priority of the Kingdom of God, the unique
authority of Jesus, the astonishing free grace of God
extended to the undeserving—and all of it a contradiction
of the Pharisees' philosophy of salvation by religious merit,
with their judging of people by external criteria—what you
wear, customs you follow, rituals you perform, and so on.
You see what I mean by Jesus the theologian? We westerners
with our logic and our analogies think of Paul as the supreme
thinker and theologian. He represents the great arguments
—the doctrines of grace—and then we go back to the
Jesus-narratives and parables for illustrations. But they are
not the illustrations. They are the theology. Paul's doctrines
are the illustrations!'

'You mean the miracles, for example, were truth in
action—God's sovereignty, the Kingdom's coming, Christ's
compassion?' I ventured.

'Yes, that—but more than that. The *parables* were theological acts as well. They revealed stunning facts about God
and his Kingdom, making such an impact that people were
changed by them. A parable was, for the hearer, an
encounter with God's ways—an encounter with God himself. People would react with anger, incredulity, joy,
amazement, hilarity, or tears. Sometimes just with silent
bewilderment. But they couldn't be the same again.'

I mused as we finished our scratch meal and strolled
back towards Bethlehem. Often, I recalled, a parable arose
out of a scene which already had controversy and drama in

it. The delightful little tale of the two debtors, for example (Lk 7:41–43). I've often preached from it, seeing it as an illustration of justification by faith and salvation by grace. But of course Kenneth Bailey was right. It wasn't just an illustration, it was the thing itself. Some of the details I knew from Edersheim.[3] Others I now checked with Kenneth. It is interesting to take a look at the complete passage in which this parable appears (Lk 7:36–50) to get a better idea of its context.

Simon the Pharisee invited Jesus home to a meal, presumably after hearing him preach. The room would be open along one side to the passing public. *First shock:* the host provides his guest with no water and no foot-washing. That was not an oversight, but, a calculated insult. Simon hadn't enjoyed the sermon! *Second shock:* a woman in the crowd following, is incensed by the insult. *She* has presumably been deeply moved by Jesus' preaching. She pushes in and takes over the neglected duty. Tears of gratitude and penitence provide the missing water, and her hair does duty for the missing towel. But, for a woman to unbind her hair is an intimate action, performed only before her husband in the bedroom. Onlookers look embarrassed, hiss and avert their eyes. *Third shock:* she produces perfume which she has been carrying. Its purpose is normally to attract customers—for she is by this time recognised as one of the community's prostitutes (known to everyone in a small town, reviled, loathed, unclean, and of course quietly used). *Fourth shock:* Simon is revolted and angry. But Jesus, looking into her eyes, and addressing her, not Simon, praises her action and condemns his inaction. *Fifth shock:* He tells a simple parable which, in its Eastern idiom announces two amazing facts. She has found God's free forgiveness, and Simon the righteous is still in his sin. Love and goodness spring from free pardon.

New light on the Prodigal Son

Later, in a study-group for Anglican workers, we sat breathlessly whilst Dr Bailey gave a more detailed demonstration.

We looked at that most famous of parables: the Prodigal Son (Lk 15:11–32). It is, of course, the parable of free forgiveness. And therein lies a problem. Those who dislike the evangelical understanding of forgiveness at a price (the price of the cross) are quick to point out with glee that it cannot be found in this parable. The runaway is forgiven simply because he is sorry and comes home. There is no mediator, no atonement, no saviour. The price of the lad's folly is paid by him, amongst the pigs, and in the reality of his repentance.

'*Wrong*,' said our instructor, and continued his riveting exposition of the Prodigal's story. (I paraphrase from now onwards, but all of this and very much more can be found in one of Kenneth Bailey's scholarly books.[4])

> Put the story back where it belongs; back in the peasant village; and it becomes the story of the Father's suffering.
>
> Remember community solidarity again. The son's demand for his inheritance before his father's death was a devastating insult to his father and a crude defiance of the whole extended family of villagers. [Every peasant community questioned by Bailey agreed.]
>
> First, the request meant in effect, 'drop dead, dad.'
>
> Second, the father should have replied with a blow on the face and a public statement, 'From now on *you* are dead.'
>
> Third, the whole community would take scandalised action. A custom called *qesasah* made provision for 'cutting off' any villager who sold his inheritance to Gentiles (which is what the son did in the far country).[5]

Consider a later stage in the story. The young man is in dire need. He comes to his senses and decides to return rather than starve. He has two problems to face. His father has been insulted and robbed by him, in a manner specifically forbidden by Jewish law. ('I have sinned against heaven and against you.') Maybe he can do something about that. He will offer to work as a hired servant (living in the village, but not at home.) His wages can gradually be saved to at least partly repay his debt. ('Make me like one of your hired men.') It is a perfect example of the Pharisees' understanding of repentance, which is essentially salvation by works—you earn God's forgiveness by prayer, almsgiving and repentance (Midrash on Psalm 18). Simon the Pharisee would have approved of the lad's new intentions so far!

So the problem of the father may perhaps be settled that way. The problem of the village really has no answer: it will just have to be faced.

Word of his return will flash around, carried by those inevitable small boys who can still gather a riotous crowd in a Palestinian village today before the sighted stranger can reach its boundary. A mob will gather with shouts, ribald threats and blows. He will have to run the gauntlet, in fact. He could even be killed.

What actually happens? The father sees his prodigal returning, and runs out of the village to meet him. *He* runs the gauntlet, to give his protection to his son. But an oriental man of property *never* runs: to do so is grievously to demean himself in society's eyes. Moreover, running is only physically possible by hitching up his tight ankle-length robe and revealing his long underpants! Shouts of anger turn to hoots of ribald mirth in the crowd. The father is suffering for the wanderer.

They meet, and the son begins his 'let's make a bargain: I'll start to work and pay' speech. The father interrupts it with wordless kisses, the gift of his own festal robe, the presentation of his own signet ring, and an order for sandals to be put on his feet. The robe would symbolise to any oriental audience imputed character, the ring delegated authority, and the sandals a promise that the youth who last 'time went out in shame from his father will soon go out on commissions for his father. I have several times preached a sermon solely on those three articles and seen lives radically changed by the implications. A converted jailbird immediately took up the point of the sandals, returned to the prison as a visitor, and led three inmates to Christ. 'I've been wearing the shoes, like you said,' he reported to me.

The community is still to be reconciled. By now the villagers will be stunned into amazed silence. Father orders an animal to be slain. Killing an animal for the sake of a guest goes far beyond mere hospitality. It is a 'blood covenant' between host and guest. The guest physically steps over the blood at the threshold, into a sacred unbreakable covenant-relationship, witnessed by the village.[6] Moreover, the killing of a small cow (food for a hundred people) is an invitation to the whole community to join in the feast that follows. The father's public words, 'you are alive' when he should have said 'you are dead' are now fortified by a command to the whole village, 'Come and join in the great reconciliation.'

Which neatly brings the end of the parable back to its beginning, which was a scandalised complaint by the Pharisees that Jesus 'welcomes sinners and eats with them' (verses 1–2). Gospel and church are here: Ephesians 2 illustrates it, but Jesus has already theologised it.

The rabbi from Nazareth has presented, in almost shocking form, a totally new concept of repentance. It is the acceptance of a completely free and undeserved offer of pardon, sonship, and membership of God's community. The price is paid by God. Is there no cross in the Prodigal Son?

Notes

1. Rabbi Stephen Schwarzschild in correspondence with John Howard Yoder. Yoder, *The Politics Of Jesus* (Eerdmans: USA, 1972), p 37
2. Yoder, *ibid* pp 65–76.
3. Alfred Edersheim, *The Life and Times of Jesus the Messiah*.
4. Kenneth Bailey, *Poet and Peasant* (Eerdmans: Michigan USA, 1976) pp 158–206.
5. Kenneth Bailey, *ibid* pp 167–168.
6. A M Rihbany, *The Syrian Christ* (Houghton Mifflin: Boston, 1916). Quoted at length by K Bailey *ibid*, pp 186–187.

10

The Donkey And the Tank

Rita and I were doing a favourite exercise. We retraced the Palm Sunday ride of Jesus, from Bethpage, down the western slope of the Mount of Olives, across Kedron, and up to the Golden Gate. Two scenes in sharp contrast suddenly confronted us. A huge military tank, gun reversed, rumbled down the Jericho road, part of the pull-out from Lebanon. And a man rode past it on a donkey. 'Behold your king comes, meek and lowly, riding on a donkey' (Zech 9:9).

What a commentary on that extraordinary last week which began when Jesus of Nazareth mounted the lowly beast and rode with his homely entourage of country folk putting on their pathetic demo, with leafy branches their only banners. To the yawning Roman sentries it meant nothing. But here was being played out the cosmic struggle for power: the seemingly endless conflict for the loyalties of humanity. Here the Man on the donkey confronted the man in the tank—and won the crown.

Approaching the city

Jesus had walked about a hundred miles from Galilee. With three miles to go, why did he suddenly want a ride? Deliberate purpose and deep symbolism was here, as his careful instructions imply (Lk 19:29–31). Bethpage, just over the crest of the hill from Bethany, had recently become the official border of the city. Standing three miles outside the actual city walls, the little cluster of houses was the equivalent of a roadsign proclaiming, 'Jerusalem—city of the great king. Population sixty thousand. Please drive carefully—we love our children.'

There at the boundary, the king made his gesture. The Messiah was popularly expected to appear some Passover week. The prophet Zechariah (his decorated tomb visible in the valley below, then and now) had painted his poignant picture of the coming king lowly and riding on a donkey yet standing triumphant upon the Mount of Olives (9:9 and 14:4). Long before that, old Jacob, blessing each of his sons from whom a tribe would descend, had spoken enigmatically of the same humble animal.

> The sceptre will not depart from Judah
> nor the ruler's staff from between his feet,
> until be comes to whom it belongs, and
> the obedience of the nations is his.
> He will tether his donkey to a vine,
> his colt to the choicest branch (Gen 49:10).

That is a picture of prosperity and power, expressed in the simple terms of a nomad. For how prosperous is someone who can use one of his vines as a tethering-post for a hungry donkey!

King, ruler's staff, sceptre, obedience of the nations... Every Jew knew what this meant, when a rabbi-prophet, renowned for miracles that outshine Isaiah's messianic expectations, at last declares himself at the entry to the City of David.

'Behold your king!'

Looking for Messiah

Isaac (let us call him) talked to us as we walked. A Jew from Whitechapel, he had chosen to 'make alliyah' and return to Zion. Now a citizen of Israel, looking out over Jerusalem's turmoil of competing religious, political and military pressures, he opened his heart to me.

'When a Jew comes back, there are four possible ways open to him. There is *Zionism*: redemption through return to the land. We thought our problems would be over then, but they were only beginning. We have to hold the land by force and exhaust our economy to do it. Nothing is solved.

'There is *Secularism*. Most Israelis have no religion. But this turns out to be barren and empty. Our youth has a huge disillusionment problem and drugs are an epidemic.

'There is *religion*. That seems the obvious way. After all, what is a Jew, if not a religious man? But we look at religious orthodoxy and we see legalism, bigotry, harshness.

'That leaves *Messiah* as the final option. We've always said, half jokingly "When Messiah comes" meaning "probably never". Like your old English phrase, "When my ship comes in." But now we are desperate for him to come. Did you know that Israeli youths have stickers that say in Hebrew "*Messiah Now?*"

'Messiah! But you see that raises a new problem. For you cannot think of Messiah for very long, without this terrible thought arising: '*What more could Messiah be than Jesus of Nazareth is already?*' Well—as for me—I have made my choice. Recently I was baptised in the name of Yeshua H'amashiah (Jesus the Messiah). Now I have been found —for he has found me.'

No fruit on the fig-tree

We lingered at Bethany, discovering to our delight a donkey in a sloping stone-filled field, tethered by a long rope to the doorpost. We thoughtfully fingering the dusty leaves and unripe fruit of a fig-tree. It was hereabouts that Jesus performed that strange act of withering the fig-tree (Mk 11:12–14).

It puzzles the modern reader. How could it be expected to yield fruit if 'it was not the season for figs'? In fact it could and should. As soon as leaves appear, the little green nutritious 'pages' (pronounced pargees) should be there too. The season for figs is the time for picking the ripened fruit (two months or more later). But for a hungry man, the pages made acceptable food: if there were none by this time, there would be none this year. And was not the whole area renounced for its little unripe figs? Beth*page* means 'the place of little figs'. So—a name for fruitfulness, but no fruit. Hypocrisy, in fact. This is what Jesus 'curses' (although it is Peter, not Jesus, who actually uses that ugly word).

An Israeli friend led us through the garden of the Paternoster Church on the outskirts of Bethpage. So-called because of the Lord's Prayer inscribed on the walls in seventy different languages, the building hides another spectacle which most tourists miss. There is the usual succession of ruins below the church—a Crusader building from the eleventh century, a Byzantine chapel from the seventh—and then a little walled-in cave with traces of worship and burial in the very earliest days of Jewish Christianity. Here is a deeply moving possibility. Jesus had some favourite spot on the summit of Olivet where he often taught (Matt 24:3, John 8:1), with the breathtaking view of Jerusalem stretched below. Was this the place? Christians in the fourth century certainly thought so, and showed it to the mother of the first Christian emperor. Even earlier—about 230 AD—two different Christian writers describe it as Jesus' place of teaching. In that case, Bethpage was privileged indeed. Here the Son of God 'brought the true light of knowledge' as Jerome says. Here he came looking for the fruit of it—and found nothing. He had already warned in a terrible parable what happens to fig-trees that yield no fruit (Lk 13:6–9).

'Cut it down! Why should it use up the soil?' Now comes the dread sentence 'May no one ever eat fruit from you again'. God's judgement, so often, is simply to say, 'Very well, go the way of your own choice—be what you want to be,' with all the inevitable consequences of such a choice.

'The essence of God's action in wrath is to *give men what they choose*, in all its implications: nothing more and equally nothing less.' (James Packer)[1]

'There are only two kinds of people in the end: those who say to God, "Thy will be done," and those to whom God says in the end, *thy* will be done. All that are in Hell choose it.' (C S Lewis)[2]

Broken-hearted love confirms our determination to choose our own way. Bethpage had made its choice, as Capernaum, Bethsaida and Chorazin had made theirs.

Weeping over the city

The road down Olivet is steep—you lean backwards, your sandals slapping on the hot stony path as you descend. Almost always there are others making the same journey: chattering tourists, serious pilgrims, earnest students. On Palm Sunday 1985 we joined the huge crowds that lined the entire route, as an extraordinary variety of religious groups joined in the traditional procession. Catholic nuns sang German hymns and gently waved palm branches. Bearded priests swung censers and intoned their prayers. Christian Zionists carried banners proclaiming their love for Jerusalem. Some group of Arab Boy Scouts, flowing keffiyah over khaki uniforms, hammered their drums and blew discordantly on their bugles. British charismatics clapped and sang Spring Harvest songs—'Hosannah to the Son of David/Jesus the Messiah reigns'.

And—irony of ironies—Israeli soldiers stood impassively

at vantage points, Uzi sub-machine guns at the ready, eyes
flickering over the crowds. An army of occupation in Arab
Jerusalem? An army of liberation in Zion? Forefront of
American Christian Fundamentalism? Foretaste of the
Redemption of Jerusalem? Scourge of the PLO and foe of
the legitimate aspiration of Palestinians? The whole
complex, contradictory confusion of modern Middle Eastern
politics and religion was present that day, as it had been in
the Spring of 28 AD when Jesus the Carpenter-rabbi rode in.

'As he approached Jerusalem and saw the city, he wept
over it and said, "If you, even you, had only known this day
what would bring you peace—but now it is hidden from
your eyes"' (Lk 19:41–42).

This was no stiff upper-lip Westerner. Jesus was a man
who lifted up his voice and wailed, the tears coursing his
face. He knew. He anticipated the choice that would be
made. 'Jesus Barabbas', the man of violence, guerilla leader
and freedom fighter, spokesman for the oft-repeated view
that man can liberate themselves by violence; that truth
and justice grow out of the barrel of a gun; that the bomb is
more effective than the ballot. And 'Jesus Bar-Joseph', the
Prince of Peace, whose soldiers would have fought for him if
his kingdom were that kind of kingdom, but it wasn't (Jn
18:36).

And, of course, he could see the consequence. They chose
Barabbas, and the way of war. It was a choice which they
kept on repeating for the next forty years. Until an exasper-
ated Rome decided to settle the issue once and for all. Titus
and Vespasian, son and father, general and future emperor,
brought their armies to Jerusalem.

Jesus warned, 'The days will come upon you when your
enemies will build an embankment against you and encircle
you and hem you in on every side' (Lk 19:43).

So they did. Josephus once defender of Galilee against
the Romans but now the invaders' war-correspondent,
describes the scene: 'Titus was now on the march from

Caesarea. He led three legions…. He ordered the fifth to join him via the Emmaus route and the tenth to ascend by way of Jericho.'[3]

The grim silent encirclement of the city began. The fifth legion made its base camp by Herod's family-tomb (the garden of the present King David Hotel) and facing Herod's Palace (now the Jaffa Gate). Titus' famous tenth legion camped on the slopes of Scopus-Olivet, just to the north of where Jesus had stood and wept. The inexorable construction of a siege-dike began, exactly as Jesus had said.

The Christian Jews within the city knew what to do. Their Master had spelled it out. 'When you see Jerusalem surrounded by armies, you will know that its desolation is near. Then let those who are in Judaea flee to the mountains, let those in the city get out…for this is the time of punishment in fulfillment of all that has been written' (Lk 21:20–22).

Led by their bishop, the Christians did exactly that—taking refuge in Pella, across Jordan in Gentile Decapolis.

The siege which followed is described is stark realism by Josephus. The pitiable tale is unique in literature for its horrific detail. Attack and counter-attack dragged on, the hopeless inhabitants fighting each other for food, staving off one relentless attack after another, and watching horrified from the walls as prisoners and deserters were crucified around the perimeter by their captors.

> Many, as they buried the fallen, fell dead themselves…no weeping or lamentation was heard: hunger stifled emotion; and with dry eyes and grinning mouths those who were slow to die watched those whose death came sooner. Bodies at first were buried, for the stench was intolerable; later, when this proved impossible, they flung them from the ramparts into the ravines.[4]

The inevitable end came. Section by section areas of the city fell to the legions. Titus ordered that the Temple itself should be preserved, and actually made various suggestions to the defenders as to how this could be ensured. A fascinating situation, this, for Jesus had said forty-two years earlier, that it would fall, and now the might of Rome, even as they capture it, say it shall stand.

> Some of his disciples were remarking about how the temple was adorned with beautiful stones and with gifts dedicated to God. But Jesus said, 'As for what you see here, the time will come when not one stone will be left on another; every one of them will be thrown down...when you see Jerusalem surrounded by armies you will know...' (Lk 21:5–6 and 20–21).

So the prophet from Nazareth. Titus from Rome, backed by a super-power and awesome force said otherwise.

> I call on my army, on the Jews in my camp, and on you yourselves as witnesses that I am not compelling you to desecrate your Temple. If you change the battleground, no Roman will go near the holy places or violate them. I will protect the Temple for you even if you do not wish me to.[5]

Who would be proved correct? The man on the donkey or the man in the tank?

> Titus returned to the Antonia, intending to launch a fullscale attack the following day at dawn and take possession of the Temple. The sanctuary, however, had long before been condemned by God to the flames.... One of the soldiers, urged on by some supernatural force, snatched a blazing piece of wood and, climbing on another soldier's back, hurled the flaming brand through a low golden window.[6]

A messenger brought the news to Titus, who dashed to the scene followed by senior officers, and tried to bring events under control.

> But his shouts were not heard and his beckoning hands went unheeded amid the avenging fury. No exhortation or threat

could now restrain the impetuosity of the legions for passion was in supreme command.

Pretending not even to hear Caesar's orders, they threw in more firebrands...carnage spread...the heap of corpses mounted higher and higher about the altar; a stream of blood flowed down the Temple's steps, and the bodies of those slain at the top slipped to the bottom.

While the Temple was ablaze, the attackers plundered it, and countless people were slaughtered. Such was the height of the hill and the magnitude of the blazing pile that the entire city seemed to be ablaze. The Temple Mount, everywhere enveloped in flames, seemed to be boiling over from its base; yet the blood seemed more abundant than the flames. The ground could not be seen between the corpses; the soldiers climbed over heaps of bodies.[7]

The awful events of 70 AD left a scar on the racial consciousness of the Jew. It was the end of their nation. For nineteen centuries 'the wandering Jew' has been an enigma of history, scattered throughout the world, different yet indefinable—and then, unthinkably, in the twentieth century, coming back to his land and his city, impelled by the events of two world wars, the collapse of empires, the horrors of the holocaust that multiplied sixfold the terrible scenes described by Josephus.

I slipped Bible and Josephus back into my knapsack and took a spectacular photograph of the Kedron valley below the city walls. Holding hands to steady each other, we continued our scrambling descent.

On our left, behind a low wall, long lines of gravestones marked a modern cemetery. A little group of *hassidim* clustered around a new grave, rocking and swaying as they chattered their prayers, each laying a little stone on the large slab, to mark their pious visit. I recalled learning at the university that two hundred tombstones had been discovered dating back to the time of Jesus. Is that what he could have meant?

'Some of the Pharisees in the crowd said to Jesus, "Teacher, rebuke your disciples!"

"I tell you," he replied, "if they keep quiet, the stones will cry out"' (Lk 19:39–40).

A magnificent piece of oriental hyperbole? Or did he mean exactly that? 'Keep my disciples quiet on this day of proclamation, and these very tombstones will crack open, as those who have gone before me bear witness from their graves that I am king, and will soon be conqueror of death'. Not so wild as it sounds at first, for something like that happened a few days later.

> When Jesus had cried out again in a loud voice, he gave up his spirit.... The tombs broke open and the bodies of many holy people who had died were raised to life. They came out of the tombs, and after Jesus' resurrection they went into the holy city and appeared to many people (Mat 27:50–53).

We met Bishop John as we reached the last turn in the path before Gethsemane. The Mount of Olives is part of his parish (or should I say diocese?). I had come to know him well, in his dark blue robe and little fez-like hat, his ginger beard as incongruous as ever. For this bishop of the ancient Church of the East, now mainly Arab, but tracing unbroken physical descent from the early disciples in Galilee, is a Scotsman! A very fine scholar, too. We paused and discussed for a few moments the subject that is uppermost in every walk on Olivet—the Kingship of Christ.

He shared a few details of a debate he'd recently had with Jewish rabbis. Reading of the *Talmud* and other rabbinical sources had led him to suspect that a strand of ancient Jewish thinking spoke in terms of the *torah* (the Law of God) as *personal* —very much as the Book of Proverbs speaks of *wisdom*. This the rabbis had admitted, and together they had plunged into the prologue to John's Gospel where Jesus, is declared as the *word*, present with God at the moment of creation, co-equal with God, yet distinct from him, and 'The Word became flesh and lived for a while among us. We have seen his glory...full of grace and truth' (Jn 1:14).

In the time of Jesus, a raised road, simply called 'the way', spanned the lower slope of Olivet to the rising ground beyond the Kedron stream. It led straight into the Golden Gate, and thence to the Temple courtyard immediately in front of the great altar. Presumably Jesus rode this way, 'Jesus entered Jerusalem and went to the temple. He looked around at everything, but since it was already late, he went out to Bethany with the Twelve' (Mk 11:11).

Matthew and Luke telescope the next day's events and make them to appear at first sight, to be the climax of the 'triumphal entry'. But Mark is quite specific. The 'cleansing of the temple' was no unpremeditated event, performed in the excitement of a popular demonstration, rendering disorder and military intervention inevitable. Jesus looked around, confirmed what previous visits had already suggested, and laid his plans for the next day. For the moment, he was fulfilling Zechariah's vision, not Malachi's; the lowly king riding on a donkey, not the Lord suddenly appearing in his temple to purge it.

But Ezekiel's enigmatic prophecy, too, found its consummation and deepest meaning now. The present Golden Gate is only 500 years old. Below it, beneath the present soil-level, lies the gate Jesus used. The present gate is a curious place, for it is totally blocked with carefully shaped stones, apparently put there not long after its construction. Why? Tales and legends abound, passed on by Jews, Christians and Muslims. It is Arab property, and part of their 'holy place'. Visitors may walk within 200 yards of it, on the 'temple mount', but go any nearer and you will be hustled away with much gesticulation, flapping of sleeves, and scowling. With elaborate unconcern Rita wandered closer whilst I kept several people engaged in conversation—and took a much-prized picture. My friends tried it in turn and were blocked by an arm-waving Arab who earnestly explained, 'Golden Gate Muslim, Western Wall Jewish, Garden Tomb Christian!' Ah well.

Back to that blocked gate. A memory stirred, but a concordance was not available. Later at the house, I checked. Yes—how odd. Ezekiel. First of all that magnificent picture from chapter 43.

'Then the man brought me to *the gate facing east*, and I saw the glory of the God of Israel coming *from the east*.... The glory of the Lord entered the temple through *the gate facing east*' (verses 1–4).

Well, that fitted Palm Sunday, in a strange, unlooked for way. But what about the gate being blocked? Yes, here it is in the next chapter.

> Then the man brought me back to the outer gate of the sanctuary, the one facing east, and it was shut. The Lord said to me, "This gate is to remain shut. It must not be opened; no-one may enter through it. It is to remain shut because the Lord, the God of Israel, has entered through it. The prince himself is the only one who may sit inside the gateway...." (44:1–3).

Bible prophecy is a strange thing. So often its import and intention is not clear until the fulfillment comes. A donkey tethered to a vine, a king lowly on an ass, the glory of God coming through the temple gateway: Jesus and his disciples, amidst shouted songs and waving palm branches.

Of course *this* one is not the actual gate of Jesus' time. I talked to someone who had spent years studying on the spot. He showed me a remarkable photograph. Renowned for his scholarship, he had been allowed to dig one dark night outside and in front of the gate. Soon he reached the curved lintel of the original structure, and eventually the space within the ancient gateway came into view. It had been blocked up, not only with stones, but with human bones!

Two explanations were given to him. One quoted Muslim

writings (Suna 79:14) in which the gate is the symbolic entrance to heaven, so where better to bury people. Another Arab authority gave a more elaborate explanation. Muslims reluctantly concede that a Jewish Messiah-figure may come, and quite inaccurately, they suppose that he will be a priest. But in the Old Testament, no priest can cross or touch a human body, or else he will become ceremonially unclean. So, if you pack the gate with bones the Messiah can never enter! Is it as easy as that? I have news for them. It will take more than bones to keep out the King of Kings!

Our walk was over. Palm Sunday had ended with a demonstration by uniformed Arabs marching the city boundaries with blaring bands and thrumming drums: they were tolerated by Israeli authorities for this one religious occasion, but really making a thinly-veiled political point. Arabs? Yes, of course many Arabs are Christians (in name and culture, at any rate). Another facet to the complicated kaleidoscope of Middle Eastern politics. Another appeal to the figure of Jesus for support. Who was this man on a donkey, and why is it that his name is so often invoked in the cause of the tank?

Will the real Jesus stand up?

The name of the man from Nazareth occupies a curious place in Israel today. Muslims affect to admire him—but strictly as a prophet, with no divine sonship, no saving cross, no resurrection. Mormons are building a huge university in his name on that very Mount of Olives (to the fury of orthodox Jews, who parade in protest every so often). But what Mormons say about Jesus is an extraordinary hotchpotch of polytheism, polygamy and occultism, with a smooth surface overlay of biblical phraseology. Jehovah's Witnesses come to Jerusalem in large numbers, and tramp around the Garden of the Tomb. They acknowledge him as some kind of king and speak much of his kingdom—yet empty his cross of its vital meaning and deny the physical reality of his rising from the grave. Priests of ancient oriental churches chant his name in prolonged ceremonies that emphasise his remoteness and differentness and seem to divorce him almost totally from everyday human life. And Jews—what do they think?

In Israel, and amongst Israelis, Jesus is a frequent talking-point. As a Christian spending a summer term in the Hebrew University, I conversed with Jewish students about Jesus almost every day, and I never started the conversation. There was no need to. He is a talking point.

For most, the old attitude to 'That One' (name never spoken, in distaste and anger) has long since gone. The Jewishness of Jesus has been rediscovered by Jew and Gentile alike. Some see him as a Zealot leader, an apocalyptic prophet and freedom fighter. This can only be proposed by making a nonsense of our primary sources of information; the Gospel records. The man on the donkey simply cannot be turned into the driver of the tank, even by tongue-in-cheek pop-religious writers like Schonfield with his 'Passover Plot'.

Others see him as radical rabbi, in the tradition of Pharisaism at its best. There is some truth in this, but only a partial truth. It can be held in isolation only at the expense of dodging his claims to unique sonship and ignoring his resurrection.

The Dead Sea Scrolls are often appealed to by well-meaning Israeli guides as the key to understanding Jesus. But in spite of some overlap of language and thought (inevitable when the same subject is being addressed) Jesus would have been given short shrift by the Essene Community. They regarded the strictest Pharisees as easy-going libertines: what would they have made of the friend of publicans and sinners?

Joseph, an Israeli guide, had taken my friends around the country for eight days, and was visibly impressed by their joyful and simple faith (many were new Christians). He watched, round-eyed, as I served communion to them at the Garden Tomb, and nodded understanding when I courteously explained that he would not be able to eat and drink with us. Next day, exploring Emmaus, I read that lovely story once more of the two disciples who invited the stranger to their Emmaus home and only discovered it was the risen Christ when he said grace with the simple meal. I had brought some long Arab loaves, the crust sprinkled with sesame seed. We broke them into meal-sized chunks and ate them in a circle, then held hands and sang, 'He is Lord, He is risen from the dead and He is Lord'.

I beckoned to our Israeli friend. 'This is not communion —simply eating in friendship,' I said. 'Please join us as our friend.' He did so, deeply affected and in tears. 'May I say something?' he asked, 'Not as your professional guide, but as Joseph, your friend. You are beautiful people, and I have experienced your love. You say the Messiah has come. I say he is still to come. If, one day, he comes, and turns out to be Jesus, then I shall not be surprised, and all of us will be glad'.

Of course that won't quite do. But it does illustrate a changing attitude to Jesus and to genuine Christians. Marco was a middle-aged student at the University, over from America for the summer. He and his wife asked me to guide them along the Via Dolorosa, to which an archaeology lecture had made passing reference. We finished at the Garden Tomb, and they stood pensively inside in the dim coolness. 'You know, I could go for everything you say about Jesus except that he was the Son of God', Marco said. The King still rides into people's lives in Jerusalem today, and demands a response. He suddenly changed the subject.

'There are no statues here, no holy pictures—why is that? The Church of the Holy Sepulchre has them all over the place.'

I explained. 'It's a matter of the Ten Commandments.

Number one is a warning against worshipping other gods. Number two forbids us to worship the true God in the wrong way. He is spirit, and an image is bound to give an inadequate and misleading impression of him. So Protestants avoid any suggestion of image-using.'

Marco gasped. 'But that's exactly why *we* don't have images! I keep finding this—that Jews and Evangelicals often say the same things!'

'Not surprising,' I said. 'After all, we're using the same Bible.'

An Israeli in his twenties listened to me preaching on the kingship of Christ in a local church, and asked to talk to me afterwards. 'I believe everything you say,' he commented. 'I had lost my faith in God. Atheism left me empty and frustrated. One day, sitting in a Jerusalem garden, I actually saw Jesus and knew he was the Messiah.'

I stared at him. 'You mean saw with your physical eyes?'

'Yes.'

'Do you mind me asking what he looked like?'

'Well—strange—I can only say he was ordinary height but at the same time looked ten feet tall.'

'How did you know he was Jesus? Did he *tell* you he was the Messiah?'

'No—it was like in a dream—you just kind of know without being told.'

'Did the vision—appearance—dream—whatever it was—*convince* you?'

'No—I shook it off—even dabbled in Buddhism for a time—but I could never forget it. Eventually I began to read the Bible—my Old Testament and your New—I found some Jews who believed in Jesus—and then, just like anyone else, Jew or Gentile I had to repent and believe and be baptized.'

Notes

1. James Packer, *Knowing God* (Hodder & Stoughton: 1973) p 139.
2. C S Lewis, *The Great Divorce* (Collins Fountain Books: 1977) Chapter 9, pp 66–67.
3. Josephus, *The Jewish War*, BK V, Chapter 1, Para 6:40–42, pp 321–322.
4. Josephus, *ibid*. BK V, Chapter 12, Para 3:514–518, p 395.
5. Josephus, *ibid*. BK VI, Chapter 2, Para 4:128, p 410.
6. Josephus, *ibid*. BK VI, Chapter 4, Para 5:249–252, p 421.
7. Josephus, *ibid*. BK VI, Chapter 5, Para 1:271–277, p 423.

Part Four

The Saviour

In the experience of reconciliation to God through Christ is to be found the principle and the touchstone of all genuine Christian doctrine. Whatever can be derived from it is true and necessary; whatever is incompatible with it lacks the essential Christian character.

(James Denny—nineteenth century)

'Are you not thirsty?' said the Lion.

'I'm *dying* of thirst,' said Jill.

'Then drink,' said the Lion.

'May I—could I—would you mind going away while I do?' said Jill.

The Lion answered this only by a look and a very low growl....

'I daren't come and drink,' said Jill.

'Then you will die of thirst,' said the Lion.

'Oh dear!' said Jill, coming another step nearer. 'I suppose I must go and look for another stream then.'

'There is no other stream,' said the Lion.

(C S Lewis, *The Silver Chair*, ch 2)

I I

With Christ in the Garden

I don't think I have ever visited Gethsemane with dry eyes.
Its location is so certain, its associations so poignant, its
appearance so suggestive. Childhood memories of Brethren
hymns merge with pictures from illustrated Bibles.

> Gethsemane, can I forget?
> Or there thy conflict see,
> Thine agony and blood-like sweat,
> And not remember Thee?

The word 'Gethsemane' (more correctly, *Gat-shemen*)
simply means *oil-press*. The whole area of the lower Olivet
slopes was planted with olive-groves (as the name suggests)
and where graveyards or churches have left it alone, it still
is. The winter stream of Kidron (as Luke wholly accurately
describes it) only runs after the winter rains, but it is
sufficient to provide the valley floor with moisture and silt,
and make hardy olives even more fruitful than usual. Nowadays the stream is tidily culverted, and a busy road crosses
it, humming with Jericho-bound traffic. But scramble over
a broken wall, sit on a sun-warmed stone, watch the olive-
leaves rustle and turn in the breeze, and you are transported
back nineteen hundred years.

Down the steps from the Upper City, past the Pool of Siloam, Jesus walked after his last Passover meal, his bewildered disciples trudging behind him. The moon, of course was full; the valley a mixture of silver light and inky shadows. Passover 1985 exactly coincided with Good Friday, so the traditional Thursday Walk of Christians had extra significance. The various Christian congregations take a three hour walk, staggered at half-hour intervals, from a communion service at the Upper Room, down through the cobbled lanes, across Kedron and into Gethsemane, stopping to read the biblical accounts and sing a hymn at appropriate spots. Down in the deep valley we could look up and see clusters of torches as later groups zig-zagged down the slope. Snatches of their songs carried to us. 'Ride on, ride on in majesty'; 'Lest I forget Gethsemane'; 'In the cross of Christ I glory'; 'Thank you Jesus, thank you Lord for loving me'...

The route took us (as it took Jesus) past the King's Garden where Solomon piped water from Gihon Spring; trees and flowers still grow in extra profusion. He wrote his Song of Songs here, and we paused to recall those evocative words in the light of the simple, sacred fellowship meal we had just shared.

'He brought me to his banquet hall, and his banner over me is love' (Song 2:4).

A tomb loomed up on our right which we know was there when Jesus passed, for it is dated. Here, too, stands Absolom's monument (rebuilt in Jesus' time). Jewish fathers used to bring their children here, tell them the story of David's spoilt and wayward son—and give them a walloping to reinforce the need for obedience! What were the thoughts of this, 'great David's greater Son', who, in total obedience to his Father's will was soon to face agony and darkness? Zechariah's monument also stood then as it still stands today by the Kedron path. Was Jesus passing this spot when he quoted from that prophet? 'I will strike the shepherd and the sheep will be scattered' (Mk 14:26–27, quoting Zech 13:7).

Can we really kneel where Jesus knelt in the garden that will forever be associated with his 'obedience unto death'? The whole lower slope of Olivet on its western (Jerusalem) side can fairly bear the name. The Gospel writers are more specific. There was an *enclosed orchard* across Kidron. Judas knew the place because Jesus often retired there with his disciples (Jn 18:1–2). To Luke, too, it was 'the usual place' (Lk 22:39–40). Jesus paused three times in the area, first to leave eight of his disciples 'sitting here' (Mk 14:25), second leaving Peter, James and John 'over there' (Matt 26:36–37) and finally moving on himself 'a stone's throw beyond them' (Lk 22:40–41). The eye-witness memories come through powerfully.

The name Gethsemane has never gone out of use from then until now. And curiously enough, there are *three* spots preserved separately for denominational reasons, which could very easily correspond to the movement of events. A little cave called Gethsemane Grotto has a domed roof, a skylight through to the sloping garden above, and artificial cisterns, channels and rock-hewn bowls which indicate an oil-press. It is old enough to have given the name originally to the area. Later it became a Christian meeting place with stone benches ('sit here'!) and later again a Christian burial-place. Now silent brown-robed Fransiscans keep it as a simple chapel.

I sat and considered, one August morning. A visit to a younger and better-preserved oil-press nearer Bethany had already given me the clues. Olives were a staple food in Jesus' time. For Arabs, they still are. They provide nutritious food, fuel for the lamps, and oil as a sovereign remedy for many medical ailments. Life, light and healing. *But first the olives must be crushed*. A huge millstone breaks them into a mush, after which the thick liquid is poured into a bowl and a great wooden screw with a flat disc is turned into it until the pure oil runs out. Broken, crushed and pressed that we might have life and light and healing. So it was with the Son of God as he faced the ultimate horror of his suffering for our sins—'And being in anguish he prayed more earnestly, and his sweat was like drops of blood falling to the ground' (Lk 22:44).

I was remembering in my prayers, as I sat there, a relative of mine, an older man, who that day was burying his wife in far-off England. I wrote a letter before I left the cave.

'As you grieve at the funeral, I am praying for you in a place called Gethsemane. As you probably know, Jesus here faced the darkness that awaited him. Because he went into it alone, we need never be alone. I pray that you will discover the comfort of that fact.'

He treasured the letter, and showed me it, back in England shortly before *he* died. By then he had discovered its truth in personal faith, and bore quiet witness to his readiness to die.

Slightly below the cave and nearer the stream, the massive Church of All Nations stands, with its great multicoloured frontage facing the Eastern Gate of the city. Otherwise known as the Basilica of the Agony, it stands where earlier Crusader and Byzantine chapels stood. Pushing through its floor is an area of unlevelled rock which, at least since 380 AD, has been marked by Christians as the place where Jesus knelt alone. Immediately behind it a quiet garden, divided into two enclosed areas by Catholic and Russian Orthodox, marks the third spot, and embodies the garden which the imaginative Bible-reader has always envisaged. There, on Passover eve, several hundred of us knelt in the moonlight and thanked him who was obedient unto death for our salvation.

Innocence on trial

In poignant words, Peter, who witnessed some of it, described the unforgettable mien of the suffering King as he moved from Gethsemane viz Caiaphas' palace to Pilate's judgement hall.

'When they hurled their insults at him, he did not retaliate: when he suffered he made no threats. Instead, he entrusted himself to him who judges justly' (1 Peter 2:23).

The best way to understand the 'trial' of Jesus is to grasp what it should have been and then in contrast see what it was. The *Mishnah* gives the ideal of Jewish justice. The Sanhedrin (Great Council) was the supreme court. 'Mercy in Judgement' was its motto. They took the attitude that the prisoner is almost always right. Not only was he innocent until proved guilty, but he was not even on trial until all the evidence of witnesses had been given, sifted and proven. It must have been an ordeal to give evidence at all; the witness must be of good character, the details of his evidence meticulously correct and in total agreement with other witnesses whose evidence he could not listen to. In a case with possible death sentence, a night for prayer and consideration must intervene between evidence and sentence. No part of the trial could be held at night, or before the Sabbath, or before a religious festival. Finally, the prisoner must not have put to him a direct question from which he might incriminate himself, and no prisoner could be found guilty on the basis of his own replies alone.

Follow Jesus' actual ordeal, and you can now see how outrageously Caiaphas and his squalid crew broke every canon of legality and justice.

Before Annas (John 18:13–14)
Annas had been sacked from the high priesthood by the Romans, but his own family (four successive sons) intrigued successfully for the job, and the position at that moment

was occupied by his son-in-law. Annas was still the power behind the throne. A Roman saying refers to his family grabbing offices as 'Coming and going like flies on a sore'. The Jews had a saying: 'the sons of Annas take the high-priesthood, make their sons priests, their nephews temple treasurers, and their servants beaters of the people'. Annas of course, already had a score to settle with Jesus: his 'bazaar' had taken a rude shaking a few days before at the hands of this young reformer. This interview presumably happened in his private residence, or at his son-in-law's official palace. We have no details of what ensued. Perhaps the old man simply had a gloating look at the prisoner.

Before Caiaphas (Jn 18:19–23)
This encounter certainly happened at the palace. It seems to have been a kind of preliminary investigation. The high priest tried to get some facts out of Jesus 'about his disciples and his preaching'. The whole proceeding was illegal (at night, before a Sabbath, before any witnesses had spoken, and putting direct questions to the prisoner). Jesus pointed this out with quiet dignity, and took a beating for doing so.

Where in fact *was* the palace? Two possible sites are offered today. One, a stopping-place for religious processions to remember the event, is based on old religious tradition established for purely liturgical reasons. The other, excavated by Fransiscans early this century, has suggestive though not conclusive archaeological facts in its favour. Visually it is stunning, and my first visit to it was a profound experience.

We clambered up Maccabean and Roman steps from the Kedron valley. It is practically certain that Jesus descended them on his night walk from the Upper Room to Gethsemane, and was hurried up them by guards who arrested him. Inscriptions include the word *corban* (Mark 7:11). Special temple balance-weights found here all date from Caiaphas's time. The three-layered ruin stands on a steep slope, with a courtyard slightly below the entrance, and dungeons below the courtyard. One of the guides employed by the Catholic church perched on the ruins, seemed to be an American charismatic. With quiet conviction she retold the story, and we realised that we were standing by the charcoal fire with Peter, looking up to the doorway as Jesus appeared. 'The Lord turned and looked straight at Peter. Then Peter remembered...and went outside and wept bitterly' (Lk 22:61–62).

How easy was Peter's swift change from 'I shan't deny you even if the others do', to 'I never knew the man'. His volatile character and his tendency to speak first and think later no doubt played a part. He would have been totally bewildered also by Jesus' own attitude—inviting arrest and discouraging resistance. There is subtle psychology at work here too. Peter was braced to meet plotting priests and brutal guards; what he tripped over was a servant-girl who casually, perhaps jokingly, said something like, 'You're not one of *his* lot are you!' The Greek sentence implies a negative: she expected the answer, 'No, not likely!' It is the *unexpected* in temptation that so easily stumbles us: Peter is committed to irreversible denial amost before he has thought about it.

The guide took us down to the dungeons: grim, cold, silent. A whipping-post stands, gaunt and hideous. The victim's arms were tied to rings in the T-shaped pillar. Little basins scooped out of the rock at his feet would have held saltwater and oil to sprinkle on the hideous lacerations in a belated touch of medical treatment afterwards. Jesus was not in fact scourged here—that was later, in the Roman praetorium. Here, Peter and John must have been tortured on a later occasion when the Sanhedrin tried to shut them up (Acts 5:40–41). But as they awaited their flogging, they could well have crouched in the same cell where Jesus waited whilst priestly father and son-in-law conferred and the Sanhedrin gathered.

Two of the women in our party stopped at the head of the

winding stairs and burst into tears. With great sensitivity, the guide murmured to me, 'Do try to persuade them to come down. They are women with personal sorrows. Let them stand where he who bore their sorrows stood. They'll cry it out in his presence, and be better for it.' She was right. One had been recently widowed in young middle-age. The other was grieving over a broken marriage. From that day onwards there was a quiet serenity in the way they began to cope.

I've stood there often since, and never failed to sense the nearness of the Man of Sorrows. Another guide on one occasion, a little Armenian, quietly spoke of 'my Saviour' with tears running down his wizened cheeks. My own voice wobbled as, at his request, I read a few words of Scripture. He murmured to me, 'You know him too—I can tell'. The tourists that time were not confessing Christians. One of them, a big American with a stetson, said, 'Thank you for the way you read that. There was something special...I don't know...', and he walked away, shaking his head.

St Peter in Gallicantu (Latin for cockcrow) is a particularly beautiful church through which the visitor has to walk to reach the dungeons. The odd, eerie feeling of passing rapidly through different layers of history is particularly acute here. Jewish Nazarenes; Byzantine Christians, Crusader knights from medieval England and Germany; gentle French Fransiscans in the nineteenth century—all have worshipped here, all have pondered on Jesus' suffering and Peter's penitence.

Before the Sanhedrin (Mark 14:55–65)

First light would be about 4.30 am. There must have been some hasty messages sent across the city as day dawned, and the next stage of the trial began. The Sanhedrin required a quorum of twenty-three members. Awkward members like Nicodemas and Joseph could have been left out. Recent excavations have uncovered a stone inscription at the foot of the southern staircase of the temple. It bears the word *zekinim* ('elders', Matthew 27:1). This confirms the statement of the Mishnah, which describes them meeting in the Hall of Hewn Stone, somewhere in the temple precincts.

The members would sit in a semi-circle, so that each could see the reaction of the others. The case should have begun with arguments for the defence: here there were none. Every canon of legality was outraged, the 'witnesses' disagreed, and Jesus was misquoted in a manner which could have no bearing on a capital charge.

The high priest committed the final outrage: a direct incriminating question, which was forbidden.

'Are you the Messiah, the Son of God?' (14:61).

Jesus' answer is often misunderstood. It was not a prophecy of his second coming. Rather, it was a direct, deliberate claim to be the fulfillment of that divine promise which above all others had given current shape to the Messianic hope. He quoted *verbatim* Daniel 7:13–14: not Messiah on earth, but Messiah before the throne of God is pictured there. Jesus says in effect, 'At the moment I stand before you. One day you will kneel before me'.

Before Pilate (Jn 18:28—19:16)
The Sanhedrin now had the vestige of a charge against him, even if illegally reached: a false claim to Messiahship (as they saw it) could be construed as blasphemy. But they now had a new problem. In 30 AD the Roman authority had removed the Sanhedrin's right to hand down a death sentence. Pilate, the procurator, must do that. So, changing the charge from a religious to a political one, they hurried Jesus to the 'palace of the Roman governor' as John calls it.

Where was this? Probably in the hated Antonia Fortress, built into the north-west corner of the temple area. Here a Roman garrison kept order in the city. The procurator, normally resident in cooler seaside Caesarea, moved to the capital with reinforcements during the excitable and

dangerous festivals. Some recent scholars have located
Pilate's part-time residence in the palace of Herod the
Great, over the western edge of the city (today's Jaffa
Gate), but the Antonia Fortress seems more likely. Its site is
still traceable, the once great four-towered building now
replaced by an Arab school, two ancient churches and a
convent. You can still see the two remaining steps of the
flight that led down from the barracks into the Temple
courtyards. A squad of soldiers at the double could be there
in minutes when the perennial 'troubles' broke out in the
shrine. That's what happened when the apostle Paul found
himself almost lynched in a near-riot (Acts 21:27–36). He
then persuaded the officer in charge to let him make a
defence from here as he 'stood on the steps, motioned to the
crowd, and when all were silent, began to speak' (40). An
eye-witness memory if ever there was one!

Pilate was in a sticky position. Secular history throws a
flood of light on his hesitations, posturing and changeability
as Jesus stood before him. Three times already his mis-
handling of the Jewish authorities and the mob had landed
him in trouble and forced him to back off from confrontation.
Once he had tried to pillage Temple funds to build an
aquaduct. Once he forced pagan military insignia into the
Temple area but had to withdraw them again. Each incident
focuses on Pilate's tendency to try to condescend to local
prejudices whilst insisting on Roman authority.

Now the priests really put the screws on. 'If you let this
man go, you are no friend of Caesar. Anyone who claims to
be a king opposes Caesar' (Jn 19:12). Pilate was trapped in
the tangled web of his own earlier cruelties and mismanage-
ments.

The whole dramatic scene was played out in front of 'the
judge's seat at a place known as the Stone Pavement, which
in Aramaic is Gabbatha', John tells us (19:13). We must
imagine a raised dais, Roman-paved, with a portico behind,
on which Pilate engaged in his extraordinary private con-

sultations with Jesus in between public appearances to argue with the priests and the gathering mob. Guides today will show you 'Pilate's Arch', half across the narrow lane of the Via Dolorosa, and half inside the church beside the lane. Unfortunately, although the site is about right this cannot be Gabbatha, for it is now evident that the arch was built a hundred years later by Hadrian, as a triumphal arch. But the church's name Ecce Homo (Behold the man) vividly recreates the scene as the mockery of a trial, interrupted by a brief and futile excursion to Herod's residence, comes to its terrible end.

It all happened within yards of here. Knock on the door of the Convent of the Sisters of Zion, as I often have done at night, feeling like Peter persuading Rhoda to let him in (Acts 12:12–14)—and for the same reason—to attend a prayer meeting of the Jerusalem believers. You will be welcomed by gentle voiced nuns who will show you Roman pavingstones that could well be the very place where yawning soldiers awaited the outcome of the trial, and vented their anti-semitism on Jesus the prisoner by crowning him in mockery with a cap of twisted thorns. Some of the stones bear marks of the king's game—a kind of chess board on which soldiers used prisoners as the 'pawns', and mocked the winner who remained on the king's square at the end of the game. Did he stand here, patient in suffering? A monk lay face-down on the stones, lost in prayer. People I had recently led to Christ knelt, awed, and touched the stones with their fingertips. I read the story aloud, and found a lump in my throat and tears in my eyes. We sang together,

King of my life I crown thee now;
Thine may the glory be!
Lest I forget thy thorn-crowned brow,
Lead me to Calvary.

The nun nodded gently. Our Israeli guide watched big-eyed. What is it that moves these Christians to love this land, and to insist that one of its rabbis is the Son of God—and their loved friend? He commented later, 'I feel closer to the Lord through being with you and watching you'.

Who is really on trial?

The overwhelming impression of these far-off events is extraordinary. For through them all it is the prisoner who moves with the quiet dignity of conscious power. The judges are on trial. It is *their* malicious cruelties and miserable compromises that stand condemned, *their* malevolent misuse of power that has *guilty* written all over it.

Consider. Jewish religion was the highest expression of man's pious instincts. Roman justice was renowned for its fairness and competence. Confronted by the only sinless man the world has ever known, they betrayed every instinct, broke every rule, and savaged every compassionate feeling. Here were the 'principalities and powers', as the apostle Paul would later describe them. Originally part of God's creation, instruments of his will for order, they have tragically shared in mankind's fall, and been captured for Satan's purposes. And Jesus, in his steady progress to the cross, '…disarmed the powers and authorities (and) made a public spectacle of them, triumphing over them by the cross' Colossians 2:15.

So many typical expressions of power were present that long night and chill morning. The power of military might (Roman soldiers); the power of popular opinion (the morning mob at the Pavement); the power of man-made religion (the Sadducees); the power of long tradition (the Pharisees); the power of political expediency (Pilate); the power of money (Judas); the power of personal fear (Peter) —all of them familiar from today's television news-bulletin. In a very real sense, they drove Jesus to the cross. *But he won, and they lost.*

Jesus has had the ultimate victory. The powers stand,

self-condemned—as Hendrick Berkhof, fresh from Nazism's bloodstained downfall wrote, 'These are the Powers that dominate mankind and are accepted as ultimate realities. But at the crucifixion, their true nature became apparent. The weapon of illusion from which they derived their strength was struck out of their hands.'[1]

Redeeming love and suffering endured have released a *power* into the lives of millions that no dictator can enforce.

Notes

1. Hendrick Berkhof, *Christ and the Powers* translated by John H Yoder (Herald Press: Ontario, 1962) p 39.

12

What Massive Stones

To the people of Jerusalem it is simply the Wall. Other
walls there are in plenty, but only one Wall. It used to be
the *Wailing* Wall: Jews came across the world to weep and
bewail the terrible events of 70 AD. Now the wailing had
ended. They have their wall back. There it stands, massive,
rough, towering into the sky, dwarfing the human figures
that cluster at its base. The first time I went, I walked right
past it, actually failing to see it because it was so big. I was
looking for something measurable and manageable. Does
the spider actually *see* the towerblock when it creeps along a
window sill?

In fact it is not 'the wall of the Temple' as it is loosely
described. Jesus said not one stone of *that* would be left
standing, and his word was literally fulfilled by Roman soldiers who had never heard of him. They pushed burning
faggots into the cracks between the massive blocks, or
cracked them loose by hammering in wooden wedges and
pouring water on to make the wood expand.

The Kotel, in fact, is simply the western retaining wall of
the slope which Herod levelled and filled so that a wider
platform could form the base of his greatly enlarged Temple.
It was still under construction when Jesus visited it. Many

of the stones weigh up to forty tons: some touch 200 tons. How they were moved and placed is something of a mystery, and theories vary from soil ramps to rounded stones which were rolled to the spot and recut. No wonder Jesus' disciples were impressed (Mt 24:1).

One does not need to take sides politically to understand the emotions of the Israeli soldiers in June 1967. A professor told me how he used to stand on the roof of the Notre Dame Church opposite the New Gate, and gaze longingly across the 500-year-old city walls into the holy city. For centuries Jews had been grudgingly permitted to crowd into the little space in front of the Wall to pray and touch the weathered stones—often mocked and jostled by Muslims and so-called Christians as they prayed. Then from 1948 until 1967, with the birth of the modern state of Israel, there was no access, and the outer city walls became the armed and touchy front line between Jordanian and Israeli troops.

That day of June 1967, Israeli tanks swept down the western slope of the Mount of Olives (a tank was knocked out beside Gethsemane). They avoided breaking through the blocked Eastern Gate—such is the power of tradition. Fighting their way through the narrow lanes of the Muslim Quarter from Herod Gate southward, they reached the fabled place.

> The captain scrambled along the roofs to the top of the wall, where he hung the blue and white Star of David. Below, some of the men moved forward to caress the great slabs of stone. Others kneeled to pray. Others simply stared. Most of them wept.
> "It's ours," one man whispered in awe. "*Jerusalem is ours.*"[1]

The area in front of the Kotel was a tangle of ramshackle buildings, some inhabited and some empty, a wilderness of barbed wire, and also a minefield. Within minutes, the chief rabbi of the army burst into the tiny square and blew a blast on the *shofar*—the ram's horn only sounded once a year. Victorious General Moshe Dyan ordered the area cleared. His men were very enthusiastic about the project. 'Give us two weeks' hard work and you won't recognise the place,' they said. 'I'll give you two days,' he replied.

They did the job. People were evicted from tenements at twelve hours' notice. Now, a plaza can hold 30,000 people when necessary. It is a strangely emotional scene. *Hassidim* stand with their faces pressed to the wall, swaying sideways and muttering prayers. Visiting Jews from every continent reach out wondering hands to touch the stones, or slip written petitions from friends at home into the unmortared cracks between. A soldier stands shawl over head, one hand holding an open prayer-book, the other grasping his sub-machine gun. An American rabbi writes later,

> The Wall. At first I faint.
> Then I see: a Wall of frozen tears,
> a cloud of sighs, waiting for redemption.
> The ground on which I stand is Amen.
> My words became echoes. All of our history
> is waiting here.[2]

Feelings run high at the Kotel. It is not easy to be objective about a subject like this—or about scenes that surrounded that dread day of the Temple's destruction. Nor is it easy to keep calm about 1967, which Israelis see as the Year of Liberation, Arabs regard as the Year of Humiliation yet to be avenged, and some Christians see as the Beginning of the End in God's prophetic timetable.

Hal Lindsay, thickset, moustached, in slacks and short sleeves, can often be seen with video-camera or notebook, scrambling over the fallen stones, collecting material to reinforce his arguments that one June day in the lifetime of most of his readers saw the fulfilment of Jesus' words and the beginning of the last rush of events that will usher in the return of Christ.

'They will fall by the sword and will be taken as prisoners to all the nations. Jerusalem will be trampled on by the Gentiles until the times of the Gentiles are fulfilled' (Lk 21:24).

That last phrase to Linday, is the crucial one. 70 AD launched a long period of Gentile oppression of Jerusalem, he reasons. Although no one at the time could have dreamt of it, it was to continue for at least 1900 years.

The 'times of the Gentiles' run concurrently with Israel's failure to grasp the offer of its Messiah, and the consequent widening of the gospel's scope so that it is offered to all the world. 'Israel has experienced a hardening in part until *the full number of the Gentiles* has come in' (Rom 11:25).

Lindsay will point out the resemblance in these two phrases. The end of the time of the Gentiles ushers in (said Jesus) the final climax of history and then

> At that time they will see the Son of Man coming in a cloud with power and great glory. When these things begin to take place stand up and lift up your heads, because your redemption i drawing near (Lk 21:27–28).

The end of the coming in of the Gentiles will be the completion of the church's task, and the Jewish rediscovery of Jesus the Messiah. 'And so all Israel will be saved, as it i written, the deliverer will come from Zion' (Rom 11:26).

March to Armageddon

So a whole scenario is sketched out, not only by Lindsay but by so many evangelical Christians with so much vigour and panache, especially in the USA, that its acceptance ha become a test of orthodoxy and spirituality (I recall an American pastor sharing his reservations about it with me and adding 'For goodness' sake keep that under your hat my denominational headquarters would sack me if the knew').

It is a projected course of events which leads direct to
Armageddon. Jerusalem will continue to be a focus of world
crisis, stimulated by the Arab-Israel conflict, Russia's
backing of Syria, America's support for Israel, the global
importance of Middle East oil, and the oft-expressed intention of Iran and its ayatollahs one day to 'march on Jerusalem'. At a time when the Gentile Church is enjoying its
final worldwide expansion, crisis will break out in the Middle
East and Israel will be threatened. The Antichrist will
appear as a political-religious figure and for a time deceive
Israel into making a pact with him, involving the rebuilding
of the Temple in Jerusalem. This will fail, Jerusalem will
find itself besieged, and at this point the Son of God will
appear in power and glory, to defeat Israel's enemies and
usher in a Millenium of peace personally ruled by himself.
There are two versions of the role of the church in these
closing events. One envisages every Christian secretly
'raptured'—caught up to heaven before the crisis erupts—
the other believes that the church, like Israel, will have to
endure the final crisis of Tribulation.

That, I think is a fair summary of a prophetic scheme
which has made several million European and American
Christians into passionate friends of the modern State of
Israel. Mayor Teddy Kolleck, the Grand Old Man of Jerusalem, has sat on the driving seat of the 'unified city' since
1967. He enjoys remarkable support from all races and
classes. He has often pointed out the friendship of funda-
mental Christians. I once heard him tell a crowd of ultra-
orthodox *Hassidim* who were being rude to Christians, that
Israel had more evangelical friends than there were Jews in
the world.

However, I will now make my shameful confession. How
many friends will I lose? Here it comes. *I have some reservations
about this scheme*. In short, it seems to put the Man on the
Donkey inside the tank after all. It confuses Jesus with
Barabbas. It ignores what Jesus said to Pilate:

"My kingdom is not of this world. If it were, my servants would fight... But now my Kingdom is from another place."

"You are a king, then!" said Pilate,

Jesus answered, "You are right in saying I am a king. In fact for this reason I was born, and for this I came into the world, to testify to the truth. Everyone on the side of truth listens to me" (Jn 18:36–37).

Of course Jesus is coming back. It is estimated that one biblical verse in every fifteen refers to that sure promise. And when he comes next time it will not be as the man of sorrows. Every knee shall bow to him. No one will have the opportunity again to say 'We will not have this man to reign over us'. All true, and my soul thrills to the promise. *But* I cannot personally equate his coming with the repulse of missiles, tanks and jets around and over a physical city. I cannot take the language of apocalypse (a perfectly recognisable language of high symbolism) and apply it with excruciating literalness to the crossroads in the Jezreel valley which bears the name H'ar Meggido (Rev 16:16) and turn the locusts with scorpion-stings (Rev 9:3–6) into military cannon-firing helicopters hovering overhead.

Of course I believe in the Sovereign God who over-rules in the rise and fall of empires, and who is bringing world affairs to a terminus appointed by himself. Of course I see therefore the re-emergence of a nation of Israel and current events in Jerusalem in that light. Of course God has not 'finished with the Jews'. The word of a converted rabbi and Christian apostle still stand: 'Theirs is the adoption as sons theirs the divine glory, the covenants, the receiving of the law, the temple worship and the promises. Theirs are the patriarchs and from them is traced the human ancestry of Christ....' (Rom 9:4–5).

Brought up amongst the Brethren, I've always regarded the Jewish people with awe as marked out for God, have been appalled and bewildered by anti-semitism amongst so-called Christian nations, and was taught, before it eve happened, that Israel would 'go back to the land'. I can recall now the first Sunday morning after the emergence of Israel as a state in 1948: it was the subject of a rapturous sermon which I listened to on the faithfulness of God and the certainty of Christ's promised return.

Most of the Christians who actually live in Jerusalem share these convictions and walk with a perpetual sense of awe. This is *his* city. He *will* stand again on the Mount of Olives. Some of them go further. They find the Hal Lindsay/ Schofield Bible scenario convincing. I've met earnest believers who have travelled to Israel at their own expense, and stand ready to be ambulance drivers for the casualties of Armageddon. One of my friends told me of tinned supplies and powdered food stockpiled in cellars, ready to feed two million Jews who will march out of Russia as Israel once came out of Egypt. I am assured by people with 'reliable sources' that the explosion of Chernobyl was actually the destruction of nuclear war-heads whose rockets stood in Syria aimed at Israel and I'm very much inclined to believe it. I am astonished and impressed by the fact that Chernobyl is the Ukranian word found in the book of Revelation: 'a great star, blazing like a torch, fell from the sky on a third of the rivers and on the springs of water—the name of the star is Wormwood' (Rev 8:10–11). Another word for Wormwood is bitterness or, in Ukranian, Chernoble.

That as I say, is the attitude of most Christians in Jerusalem. But they have a cautious attitude to literal and melodramatic theories about the fulfilments of age-old prophecies. Jesus Christ is Saviour for all—Jew and Gentile. His Church is a universal brotherhood in which there is no place for racial division. As a matter of sober fact, there are more Christians in Russia than in Western Europe. Syria has probably the largest Evangelical church in the Middle East—most of its members being, of course, Arabs. A possible rebuilt Temple fails to excite me: Jesus has announced that as far as worship is concerned, mountains are off and temples are out (John 4:19–24). What would anyone do with a temple when the final sacrifice for sin has been offered, accepted, and proved gloriously and eternally efficacious?

What kind of kingdom?

We opened the 'Jerusalem Post' one morning, and read that Israeli planes had flown across North Africa and bombed Tunis. Within hours, well-meaning Christian expatriates had sent an 'open letter' to the Israeli government expressing Christian approval and understanding. Next day the local evangelical pastors met, and not one of them approved of that message. It certainly did not represent the views of any Christian congregation in the city. To approve or disapprove the violent actions of a sovereign state in the Middle East is irrelevant to the gospel Christ came to make possible and the Kingdom that Christ came to establish. These pastors live amongst Jews, Arabs, Greeks, Germans, Americans. They serve and proclaim a Saviour who won the victory over sin by suffering without resistance, who wins men's hearts by the power of redeeming love, and who is building his church across every racial and national barrier.

Most Christians, their minds stored with Bible incidents and precedent, instinctively love the land where God has uniquely acted for the world's salvation. They watch with awe the saga of the Jewish people, whose continued existence seems to bear witness to the promises of God. Those who know it blush with shame at Christendom's treatment of the Jews. I talked to an Israeli from the Warsaw ghetto, now an aged follower of Jesus. It is a miracle that he is. He told me how, in the 1930's Jewish children hid in terror on Good Friday, as gangs of 'Christian' youths rampaged the streets beating up 'the Christ-killers'. To the average Jew, 'Christianity' is a national and cultural phenomenon:

Europeans are Christians, just as Arabs are Muslims and Jews are Jews. So were the Nazis Christians. The Crusaders were Christians. The Klu Klux Klan are Christians. The Inquisition was an arm of the Church. We Christians have a lot of fences to mend.

Christians who today express love and admiration for the Jew and for Israel are met by Jews, first with incredulity, and then with tears of joy. Dialogue between the two has become commonplace. I was asked to conduct a group of Israeli professors and their wives around some of the Christian holy sites. When we came to the Garden Tomb I said, 'It is impossible for me, as a Christian, to speak of the crucifixion without also speaking of the resurrection. That, I know, is unacceptable to you, but let me simply stick to the record, and give my reasons for believing it'. One of them piped up, 'Say what you like. Your respect, your humour and your humanity speak for you.' The others nodded and murmured agreement.

A Jewish businessman and his wife invited me to a meal. They talked of the Holocaust. Six million Jewish men, women and children murdered! Had I any comment to make about a God in whom they tried to believe in spite of *that*?

'Have you ever studied the Suffering Servant in your Scriptures?' I asked. They hadn't.

'You'll find him in the book of Isaiah. It isn't easy to see who the prophet is referring to. Sometimes he seems to mean simply the people of Israel, sometimes a kind of ideal Israel—what you *ought* to be. But he says something very strange which bears on the Holocaust. This world is such a sinful world that the more goodness a man displays, the more hostility he arouses from the world around. As a matter of fact Plato said that, too. Imagine a perfect man, if such were possible. He would show up the world's faults so powerfully that they would 'bind him, scourge him and finally impale him,' Plato suggested. Now—Isaiah seems to say something very similar. In a way, the more the Jew is faithful to his God, the more he will attract hatred, evil, cruelty. In a sense, then, the 'just' (comparatively speaking) will bear the sins of the 'unjust'.

I paused. The two of them were fascinated. 'Go on,' said the husband. His wife slipped her hand into his.

'Now—what happened during the Holocaust? Nazism was displayed in all its horror, Fascism was displayed as the evil thing it is. Anti-semitism, so shamefully nursed by so many, was exposed in all the evil of its final logic. The world shrank from it, condemned it, disowned it.'

I drew a careful breath and went on, 'Now forgive me saying this next thing. What if there were not merely a *good people* but a *perfect man* from amongst that people. Well—Isaiah believed there would be. And this is what he says will happen.'

(I began to quote, from memory, and therefore from the King James version).

> He was stricken, smitten and afflicted.
> He was wounded for our transgressions and bruised for
> our iniquities.
> The chastisement of our peace was upon him,
> and with his stripes we are healed. (Is 53:4–5).

'Isaiah says that?' asked the wife. 'You know, we Jew hardly ever read our Bible. I've often thought how odd it i that Christians know it better than we do.'

'Well the words are there, certainly. And, you see, m part-answer to your question about God and suffering i that I don't have a complete answer, but I believe the key i held by the greatest Jew who ever lived—a suffering Jew who to me is the suffering Saviour!'

Jesus Christ is still the issue between Jew and Christian as he is between Christian and Muslim. In the words of tha same prophet, he is the stone on which each of us rises to th heights—or stumbles and breaks his leg. That does no mean that we need to get angry or condemn each other. He is greater than any of us—greater than any of the words we find to say about him. An Israeli scholar who is a household name in Israel said to a Baptist friend of mine (also a scholar), 'I have gradually come to the place where I can acknowledge Jesus to be the Son of Man portrayed in the seventh chapter of Daniel. What I cannot do is use the philosophical categories of the Roman and Greek Church of the second to fifth centuries as a model description of him.' Well—how many Western Christians can recite the Athanasian Creed? Even less can *understand* it! I'm glad that I can safely leave God to decide where that man stands in his sight.

I personally cannot believe that we will draw Jews to the authentic Jesus by forcing him back into the literal mould of a conquering king. With the best intentions in the world some Christians showed a film around Jerusalem which drew on grim pictures from Ezekiel, interpreted with blood-thirsty literalness, to forecast a Russian invasion via Syria into Israel, and promised that Jesus would return to rescue them. Will the man on a donkey really become a man in a tank?

However, much more in the spirit of the New Testament, ironically, is the German-Jewish theologian, Pinchas Lapide who has written a book on the resurrection of Jesus. He musters the evidence that the resurrection took place—the classic arguments that evangelical Christians have employed so often. He then asks what this implies. Since Jesus clearly rose from the dead, must he not be the Son of God and the Messiah? Rather, Lapide suggests, Christ's ministry, death and resurrection were 'Messianic events'. Consider the Holocaust, he suggests. Its agony and death led to a resurrection, for out of it came the birth of the State of Israel, and a witness to the world. Might it not be that the Jews failed to acknowledge Jesus, and thus his death and resurrection became a means whereby the knowledge of the

God of Israel was taken to the Gentile world?[3]

That is so like Paul's argument that it takes one's breath away.[4]

An over-zealous American tourist asked his Israeli guide, 'What will you say when Messiah comes, and proves to be Jesus?' The guide paused for a moment, and then asked, 'What will you say when Jesus comes, and proves to be a Jewish Rabbi?'

What indeed?

Notes

1. Clifford Irving, *The Battle of Jerusalem* (Macmillan: London, 1970), p 68.
2. Rabbi Abraham J Heschel, quoted by Elisabeth Elliot, *Furnace of the Lord* (Hodder & Stoughton, 1969), p 9.
3. Pinchas Lapide, *The Resurrection of Jesus* (SCM Press).
4. Epistle to the Romans 11:11–25.

13

Witness of the Empty Tomb

One of the guides grabbed my arm. 'I'm sure that's George Taylor!' 'Pardon?' 'George Taylor! You know—one of the Magnificent Seven. Remember those marvellous cowboy films that made Yul Brynner famous. That's the one that shot the noose off his friend's neck just as they were hanging him!'

He was right, too, my friend with the encyclopedic knowledge of Hollywood westerns. I recognised the man myself now, although I didn't recall the incident of the noose. Very big, a splendidly brutal face, and legs that looked positively odd without a horse between them. He and his slim blonde wife asked me to show them around, and soon we were inspecting the wine-press, looking out over skull hill, stooping to enter the tomb. As we came out again, blinking in the sunshine, I said, 'Of course we can't guarantee that this is the very place. And it really doesn't matter. Nothing depends on finding *where* Christ died—everything depends on discovering *why* he did it.' I glanced at them to see their reaction, and gently pushed a little harder. 'Even the arguments for the resurrection, although very impressive, can never be wholly conclusive. There has to be faith. In the long run it's like this: an old hymn poses the question, "You ask me how I know he lives...."' The film star's wife interrupted with a big grin and finished the quotation for me 'He lives within my heart!' She squeezed her husband's arm: 'And he does, too—he lives in both of us.' I laughed with delight, and we all hugged each other. Just another incident in the seemingly endless succession of passing encounters at the Garden Tomb.

The apostle Paul once said on a dramatic occasion, 'I stand here and testify to small and great alike...that the Christ would suffer and (be) first to rise from the dead' (Acts 26:22–23).

Our circumstances were very different, but the purpose was the same. Bishop Arthur Goodwin-Hudson used to describe the Garden Tomb as 'the world's greatest Gospel visual-aid.'

There, life-size, was an execution site outside Jerusalem's city wall, a skull-shaped hill, a rich man's garden, a rolling stone tomb. People came in their hundreds; individuals and families, pilgrimages and tour-groups, twenty at a time, two hundred at a time, often over a thousand in one working day. All heard the gospel story in its simplicity.

American sailors on shore-leave, European school-children on a Mediterranean cruise, church groups led by pastors and priests, United Nations peace-keeping troops from Sinai and Golan, Japanese businessmen, Africans in gorgeous flamboyant robes, West Indians who have rushed back to the hotel to dress in white before coming to the garden—in they poured, round they walked, whispering, chattering, singing, staring...sometimes crying.

At one level we were simply a tourist-trap, a point on most people's itinerary because we qualified for that curious accolade, an Israeli government 'registered holy site'! At another level, without any deceit, we operated as a gentle evangelistic agency that contented itself with simply stating the historical facts, illustrating them visually, and answering people's questions. Peter's well-known words (one of my mottoes since teenage years) really summed it up. 'Always be prepared to give an answer to everyone who asks you to give the reason for the hope that you have...with gentleness and respect' (1 Peter 3:15–16).

One day, for example, our son Paul was taking round an American church group. The area around the tomb was crowded as they approached, so he stood by the wine-press and said, half-jokingly, 'We shall have to wait here for a few minutes: if it was a big longer I might preach you a sermon!' The group-leader piped up 'Why not?' Paul spoke for five minutes on the meaning of the words 'Christ died for our sins', and finished with 'In the long run, what matters is not the site of the empty tomb, but a sight of the One who left it empty.'

Two girl hikers, drifting around the youth hostels, had listened from the edge of the crowd. Pushing forward, they asked how they might commit their lives to Christ.

Living in very different style was the visiting group of politicians and businessmen from an American state— Jewish and Gentile. The state governor was one of them, and we had to make quiet 'security' arrangements for them to look around privately. Some of them wished to stay for the open-air service held weekly. One of the governor's security agents seemed new to the job: he spent much of the sermon buttoning and unbuttoning his jacket, and easing his gun in and out of its shoulder-holster. Suddenly there was a very loud bang. It often happens: Israeli fighter-planes patrolling the Jordanian border, sweep up over the Judaean wilderness and break the sound barrier. People unaccustomed to it do have a tendency to dive for cover. Several in the congregation did so now, and the nervous agent did a splendid Starsky and Hutch imitation, leaping in front of the governor, knees in crouch position, arms out stiff, automatic pistol held two-handed.

It did tend to interrupt the flow of the sermon, which was entitled 'Jesus—the Man we cannot ignore'. I paused and explained. 'Don't be distressed. If you hear a loud bang, always listen for the sound of an aeroplane afterwards. If you can hear it, there's nothing to worry about. If you can't hear anything, it's too late!'

There was a lot of hearty laughter, the agent sheepishly put his gun away, and the sermon continued. Afterwards, one of the party, proprietor and editor of a major American newspaper, told me, 'This morning I have rediscovered my childhood faith. Thank you. If you ever come to the States, I'd like you to visit with me.'

I wasn't too sure what that peculiarly American phrase 'visit with me' meant, but when I took him up on it a year later I found myself as his guest, invited to speak to the civic and business heads of a famous city. One of them testified to the others that his life had been completely 'changed' by that visit to the garden. A local Baptist pastor who took me to the meal whispered, white-faced with excitement, 'Do you realise what you've got here? The financial, political and social power of this city.'

It led to more—a great deal more at a higher level still, but name-dropping is not my concern. 'I testify to small and great alike....'

The Anglican writer and preacher D R Davies used to describe the church sermon as 'twenty minutes to raise the dead'.

We normally had about five minutes more than that to take a group around the site, explain the natural features, the archaeological arguments, the historical facts—and to show how God did in fact raise the dead. Sometimes it was a good deal less. Everyone has heard of those lightning tours so beloved by Americans. One party leader wrote to me recently with the outline of a proposed Christian Heritage Holiday in Britain. It included for Day 2 (I quote) 'Tour of Ireland, ferry to Scotland, preliminary tour of Scotland....'

Some of the Mediterranean tours are rather like this. They include a ship's arrival in Haifa, and a day's tour of

Israel. Two hours are given (disproportionately) to Jerusalem. The Garden Tomb gets ten minutes, and as we had the city's cleanest 'washrooms' (as the Americans call toilets) there was usually a rush for them.

I never actually heard an Israeli version of the fabled phrase, 'It's Tuesday so this must be France', but I do recall one lady who trudged up the path with her lightning-tour group, and asked me dazedly, 'What country is this?'

We usually managed to negotiate fifteen minutes *plus* the washroom visit. Was it worth it? Some of our governing committee doubted it. But after all, words of Scripture form the living Word of God, the divine seed that produces life in the responsive heart. Even very small seed can produce a very big plant, as Jesus illustrated from the parable of the mustard seed (Matt 13:31–32).

We grew that tree at the garden, and I would often pass the tiny seeds on to visitors and silently pray that the few words I said would have the same effect. When it did, we sometimes heard: more often we knew nothing of the harvest.

During the heat of the summer, when few tourists come, I flew home to Britain and preached at the Keswick Bible Convention. One lady there told me a story.

'Four months ago I was on one of those whistle-stop Mediterranean tours. I found, to my embarrassment that most of the passengers were high-spending and hard-drinking brewers and their wives. We had one day in Israel, and I asked the guide to show us the Garden Tomb. He refused, but several couples became curious, and insisted and we went to see it. Five days later, in an Athens hotel, some of us were sitting in the hotel lounge discussing the holiday and what had impressed us most. One wealthy woman said, "Well that missionary place, the Garden Tomb, interested me more than anything else. I won't forget it for a long time." A brewer's wife quietly chipped in: "I shan't *ever* forget it. It has changed my life. I became a Christian while we were there".'

At the same Convention, a group of Christians from Cornwall told me, 'A wealthy woman from our little village came back from a Holy Land holiday last winter. She amazed everyone by telling them that she had become a convinced Christian through visiting the Tomb. She has plunged into all kinds of witnessing, and has already made a real impact on the district.'

Worship the King

Of course many were already convinced and committed before they came. I estimate that half of the thousand-a-day are evangelical or charismatic Christians, who make the visit to the Garden Tomb the high point of their tour. Half a dozen large and small worship areas are landscaped into the one-acre garden, usually grouped around a stone communion table. All six will often be in use at one time, and the murmur of prayers, the reading of Scripture, the singing of hymns in several different languages, mingle in the air with a quiet harmony that seems to signal that Pentecost has stood the Tower of Babel on its head and given all believers one common tongue of prayer and praise. Words like *Hallelujah* and *Jesus* sound very much the same in French, Chinese, Polish and Swahili!

A huge black man with gleaming teeth, a gold crown on his head, a purple robe and an orange cummerbund, introduces himself as the Archbishop of the Marching Church of Zimbabwe with Signs Following. The worship of his group is a fascinating mixture of Anglican liturgy and charismatic improvisation; at one point they dance in an opening and closing circle, the men stamping their feet and the women ululating: it is like a scene from Rider Haggard. In contrast, stolid German believers sing a sombre hymn with lovely humming harmony that I suspect comes straight from Martin Luther.

A large party of Japanese from some new sect ask if they

might hold a service in front of the tomb. I use my discretion, and suggest they come at lunchtime when the Garden is closed to visitors: someone has warned me they are rather noisy. That proves to be something of an understatement. I have never heard a cacophony quite like it: hooting, babbling, shouting. It actually brings Arabs running up the lane and climbing the wall on each other's shoulders, to see what's going on. I have given them thirty minutes, but wonder how ever I am going to stop them. No need to worry.

Exactly on the dot, their leader glances at his watch, shouts a word of command and instantly, in full flight, surely halfway through a sentence, the noise stops. They smile, march out silently, and hand me a box of chocolate biscuits from Japan with much bowing. Bemused, I slip into a returning-the-bow routine, in true Peter Sellers fashion, and realise that the only way to bring it to an end is for me to stop. My son falls around laughing in the background, and a new joke is added to the impressive family record.

Humour is a great releaser of tension. We are catering for considerable numbers of people, a good percentage of whom show all the unreasonableness, bad manners and outrageous demands that any shop assistant experiences. The twin gift of keeping cool at the time but turning each bad experience into a joke afterwards is very necessary. Once the gate was closed, we would sometimes be bursting to relate incidents, and tease each other for the way we handled or mishandled them.

There was the man with the flowing beard and big stick who sometimes stood just outside and silently gave out religious tracts, but now and again had spells in which he seemed convinced that he was Elijah, and would come inside to shake his cudgel at us and call us 'paper Christians'.

There was the American televangelist who arrived with two hundred followers, four carrying a coffin-like box full of prayers written on slips of paper. 'A thousand who could not come here paid ten dollars each to have their prayers read at Calvary' he said. He got short shrift.

The Garden Tomb Association specifically protects the area from 'commercialism and superstition', and we have the same aim so we coldly pointed out that Calvary (if indeed skull hill is that) stands outside our garden, in the Arab bus-station. We discover afterwards that the evangelist has stood on the city wall 200 yards from the cliff, and with some artful camera angles has contrived to give the impression that he is 'at Calvary'. It is, after all, the image that counts. And the dollars, of course.

A group of Caribbean Christians poured in—lovely, simple, happy people. All of them were very heavily built. Our guide finished his peroration with his favourite words, 'Let me tell you the most wonderful thing about the tomb of Jesus wherever it is—*it is empty!*'

The most buxom lady in the crowd let out a whoop of '*Hallelujah!*' turned an astonishing cartwheel, then attempted a second one, and landed upside down in a flowering shrub, legs waving in the air. Hauled out by her friends, she smiled placidly as if nothing had happened, and gave her attention to the last few words from the startled guide.

One of us explained to a quiet group of Canadians that this *may* be the Garden of Joseph of Arimathea. A lady interrupted to ask, 'Wasn't that the one with the coat of many colours?' 'No dear,' intervened her husband, 'He means the man that started the Mormons.'

My son, in clowning mood, with a particularly friendly group, decided to tease them. He said solemnly, 'One very impressive proof we have found is a tree with a heart carved on it, and the words, "Joseph loves Mrs Arimathea"'. A few chuckled, but Paul had the feeling that the joke didn't click. After their walk, one minister's wife came to him perfectly seriously and asked to be shown the tree—she'd love to have a photograph!

Two of the staff overheard a particularly brilliant piece of
tact from me (they assure me with gasps of mock-admira-
tion). Someone had asked me if General Gordon still lives
here (he died just over a hundred years ago). I gravely
explained that 'The Gordon family are not directly respon-
sible for the Garden nowadays.' I definitely won the current
award for Answer of the Week.

Someone else was very insistent that last time he came,
ten years ago, he heard General Gordon preach here. At
first he got quite vexed at my suggestion that this wasn't
possible, but we avoided further argument when I wondered
aloud whether it might have been Colonel Dobbie, and he
acknowledged that it could have been. It was a soldier,
anyway.

The inevitable know-all who has been before kept assur-
ing his friends that the whole thing was a con-trick; it
appeared that we had altered the layout since he last came.
In fact we have had to widen and reroute one of the paths
because of increasing numbers of visitors. He seemd to
think that someone assured him last time that the body of
Jesus was carried along this very track. Now he suddenly
asserted that we had 'moved the stone'. I pricked up my
ears, for Morrison's splendid book *Who Moved the Stone?* is a
favourite of mine. 'You mean the stone from the door of the
tomb? No, we've never had that there—it wasn't found in
1867, when the tomb was rediscovered.'

'Nonsense,' shouted the pest. 'It was here ten years ago, I
tell you. You've altered everything.' 'Tell you what,' I
suggested, 'When you get home, look up your holiday
snaps. If you can find one with the Stone on it, send me it in
the post, and I'll pay you fifty dollars for it.' He seemed
satisfied, and of course, I never heard from him again.

Curiously, at least twenty people have assured me at
different times that they saw the rolling-stone last time they
were here. Possibly they have confused memories of the

Herod family tomb on the western slope of the city, a fine example of this kind of tomb, and one of the very few discovered in Israel. Most people were buried in a *kokh*. The Hebrew word means 'oven', and refers to an oven-like aperture cut out of the rock, just large enough for a body to be slid horizontally into it. The little opening was then blocked with stone and clay. But the Gospel records speak clearly of a large vaulted tomb for Jesus' burial (Jn 19:41) having room for several people (and angels!) to stand inside, and closed with a 'great stone' (Matt 27:60). This is exactly in accord with what we know of a rich man's burial, and of course, Joseph of Arimathea, a member of the ruling Sanhedrin, was a wealthy man.

The stone could be held in place by a number of different devices; at Herod's Tomb an arch holds it in place; at the Garden Tomb a low sloping wall about nine inches high runs across the doorway, eighteen inches in front of it and slightly bevelled. The stone itself was no doubt bevelled around the outside edge to fit this shape. Dame Katherine Kenyon, the British pioneer archaeologist who confirmed the approximate dating and style of the Garden Tomb, calculated that the stone itself was unusually large. It probably stood seven feet high, eighteen inches thick, and weighed about seven tons.

These impressive figures are important. One of the earliest 'explanations' for the undoubtedly empty tomb was the charge that the disciples moved the stone, stole the body, and then pretended that Jesus had risen. Matthew mentions where the story came from; the Sanhedrin bribed the guards to 'admit' that they fell asleep on duty and the disciples took that opportunity. We have independent evidence of this story in the North African world of the early second century, where Tertullian, the converted lawyer, came across it before the New Testament was bound together and distributed as the Christian Bible.

I once took a large crowd of Ghanian UN soldiers to the

tomb entrance, and gave them a short lecture on evidence for the resurrection. 'do you know what the penalty was for a Roman soldier sleeping on duty?' I asked.

There was a buzz of speculation, and then I told them.

'It was crucifixion upside down. Can you imagine them going to sleep with *that* hanging over them? The Bible uses a technical phrase—there was a *squad* of them, as we might say. Fourteen. So all fourteen have to nod off. All at once, mind you—so that not one is left awake to shake the others awake again for fear of being crucified upside down.'

The tough troops saw the point clearly enough, and I warmed to my argument.

'Now take your imagination a bit further. They all have to not only nod off, but fall so deeply asleep that a gang of Galileans can come along with ropes and pulleys, block and tackle, *and move seven tons of stone without waking a single one up!*'

They were laughing and nodding now.

'Imagine those sentries giving their evidence later. The judge asks them what happened. They say that those rotten Nazarenes came along and pulled a fast one. How do you know? they would be asked. What's your evidence? And out comes the classic answer—Your honour, we know because we were eye-witnesses. We were there when it happened—er—fast asleep!'

The Africans burst out laughing, slapping each other's backs and clapping.

'You see all that story from the guards actually *proves* is that the tomb really was empty. Otherwise why give a story to account for its emptiness?'

I held out my hands appealingly.

'What have we got then? An empty tomb and a daft explanation that explains nothing. How does the *Bible* explain it? St Paul sums it up in one sentence, at the end of Romans chapter four. He says, "He was delivered over to death for our sins, and was raised to life for our justification" (Rom 4:25). I like to put it simply like this: At the cross, the

Son of God paid the price for our sins. At the empty tomb the Father wrote the receipt underneath—*Received With Thanks*. Believe that. Pin all your hope to it. Ask God to bring the power of it into your life.'

A young officer raised his hand. 'May I say something sir?' He stepped out of the crowd and addressed the others.

'Men—what this man says is true. I believe it. I'm not ashamed of it. I want you all to believe it.'

They crowded round me to look at Bible verses, to get my autograph, to ask me to pray for them, to take copies of Scripture portions.

God was at work in the Garden, touching men's lives.

Part Five

The Problem

On that day, when all the nations of the earth are gathered against her, I will make Jerusalem an immovable rock for all the nations. All who try to move it will injure themselves.

(Zechariah 12:3)

14

Prophecy, Politics and the People of God

> The battle for Israel is no modern phenomenon. Her right to exist and her claim to destiny has always been contested. From the very beginning of her history the powers of darkness and evil have sought to destroy her from both without and within.... We are witnessing in our generation the climax of that battle. It will not cease until the Lord Jesus returns.[1]

So writes Lance Lambert, a bland-featured, thickset Jewish Christian, resident of Jerusalem, friend of Israeli cabinet ministers, Christ exalting evangelist, who has come to represent the voice of Jewish-evangelical understanding in the Middle East. He is one of the finest raconteurs I have ever met: his yarns can hold me silent and open-mouthed for hours. His own adventures would sound highly unlikely if published as a paperback thriller.

But the thrust of Lambert's worldwide itinerant ministry is always the same. Israel—the land and the people—has always stood at the heart of the purposes of God. Events today point up that lesson, and send out an urgent signal to Christians everywhere to pray and plan and persevere, in expectation of the final great conflict between light and darkness. 'The presence of Israel on the contemporary world scene is a miracle...through this one small nation, the living God is speaking to the nations of the world.'[2]

It is a conviction shared by many Christians, particularly in the western world. I know American pastors who attribute the obvious blessing of God on their local church ministry to the fact that they speak out publicly in favour of the State of Israel, organise Jewish-Christian dialogue, and lead regular twice-a-year trips to Israel. God, they reason, still pledges to bless those who bless Abraham (Genesis 12:1–3).

The International Christian Embassy in Jerusalem is an extraordinary organisation committed to the same view. When Israel captured East Jerusalem and the Old City in 1967 she rapidly annexed the whole area and announced Jerusalem to be 'the eternal capital of Israel'. The international community, even America, baulked at this and with the curious exception of Costa Rica, the nations insisted on having their embassies in Tel Aviv. Incensed by this, Christian enthusiasts from as far away as the USA, Britain, Holand, South Africa and Australia, organised their own 'embassy', which channels aid funds, encourages cultural exchange, publishes press-releases, and maintains dialogue with the Israelis. One of its most colourful triumphs has been to persuade thousands of Christians to visit Jerusalem during *succot* (the feast of Tabernacles) and to join in the national celebrations and marches, as well as having their own bannered and musical 'praise walk', around the Old City. A Chief Rabbi, watching one of the earliest marches, in tears said, 'Now before my eyes I see Zechariah's promise fulfilled. "Many peoples and powerful nations will come to Jerusalem to seek the Lord Almighty"' (Zechariah 8:22). Coupled with this has been a remarkable growing Christian-Jewish dialogue. If we are not *brothers* (in the fullest New Testament sense of that word) we are at least coming to realise that we are *cousins*. We share such an enormous common heritage. This is more to do with monotheism, morality and Moses than with the actual land of Palestine-

Israel, but the two things cohere so closely in the Jewish mind that Christians often find themselves sounding like Zionists in their sense of solidarity with Jews. And without doubt the re-emergence of the modern State of Israel in world headlines has created in many Christians not only a warmth for the people but an admiration for the nation. The Holocaust, the birth of Israel, the Six Day War, Yom Kippur...prophecy seems to be fulfilled before our eyes. Names and places hallowed by sermons and scriptures beckon to us across the television screens—just four hours from Gatwick Airport.

At this point international politics muddy the waters. Ever since the Second World War, Israel's enemies have coincidentally been the enemies of America and Western Europe. The Mufti of Jerusalem was a friend and imitator of Hitler. Yasser Arafat became the public face of indiscriminate terrorism in Europe. The Arab supporters of the Yom Kippur war blackmailed the west with their oil threat. The Palestinian raiders in Galilee made western type Lebanon into a mad-house of civil strife. All of this is an over-simplification (and chauvinistic too). But it does create an atmosphere in those very nations where evangelical Christianity has its roots. The Arabs have a saying: 'the enemy of my friend is my enemy, and the enemy of my enemy is my friend.' By that reckoning western Christians feel pretty clear who is their friend in the Middle East.

But it is not as simple as that. Bishop Samir Kafiti, Arab Anglican bishop in Jerusalem said bitterly to me once, 'No one west of Greece seems to know that there is an Arab Christianity, and that the Church has continued unbroken here since the apostles.' He gesticulated sadly. 'Christians come on their pilgrimages from Europe, and they spend all their time looking at Jewish holy sites. No one ever takes them to meet an Arab Christian congregation. But our Lord is not building temples today—he's building a spiritual temple in which every believer in Jesus is a living stone.

Isn't that what Peter says?' I had to admit that he had a point.

Have we western Christians become over-obsessed with the Land, substituting sentimental euphoria for hard biblical thinking, and sheltering from the reality of a universal gospel in the dream-world of apocalyptic hopes and dramatic prophecy? As I write, horrifying news filters through the TV-channels of riots on the Temple Mount, petrol-bombings in Bethlehem, shootings in Hebron, hatred in Nazareth, killings in Gaza. Behind it all are years of broken promises, cynical exploitations, vicious propaganda, political power-play, irreconcilable claims and wild rhetoric as the nations of the world have made Palestine-Israel the arena of their ideological conflict. There is guilt on both sides. And on both sides, widows weep, children suffer, and young men learn to hate and kill. Christians may be able to do little for the politics of it all, but we owe it to our own Lord who acted savingly in that Land, to do some hard thinking. This is not a book of theology, and it cannot suddenly turn into one in the last chapter. But the posing of a few questions would make a fitting conclusion.

Who is today's Israel?

The answer might seem obvious. Israel, you will say, is the new dramatic fact that has flung this century back into biblical times. Israel is that gallant little nation with its citizen-army of teens and twenties, maligned and misreported, hated and envied, that has come out of the horrors of the Holocaust, wrested a homeland from rocks and swamps, and made the desert blossom like an orchard. All true. *But is that what the New Testament means by 'Israel'?* The apostle Paul argues that God's Israel should not be confused with the mere State of Israel. 'Not all who are descended from Israel are Israel. Nor because they are his descendants are they all Abraham's children' (Rom 9:6–7).

He goes on to argue that those who display Abraham's faith in Abraham's God are Abraham's children. It is a theme that runs throughout the teaching of Jesus himself (Jn 8:31–39, Matt 21:33–46). It is caught up by the apostles (1 Peter 1:4–10, James 1:1, Gal 3:6–9). Moreover the New Testament insists that this was the message of the prophets too. Notice how James settles the dispute as to whether non-Jews can enter the church, by quoting the prophecy of Amos, 'In that day I will restore David's fallen tent' (Amos 9:11/Acts 15:1–19).

This is vital to grasp. We shall get into a fine muddle if we automatically equate every biblical reference to Israel the people of God with Israel the modern political state. Incidentally, many religious Jews inside and outside Israel recognise that. Some of the *hassidim* do not recognise modern Israel as God's Israel at all, and decline to pay its taxes or serve in its army. Only Messiah can create Israel, they insist.

Now another question that follows logically.

Who are the people of God today?

The New Testament gives a clear answer: not the Jews. Not the Gentiles either. But *the worldwide Church*, made up of believers reborn into living relationship with God. The Bishop in Jerusalem was right in his remark. God is making one people, Jew and Gentile alike, Israeli and Arab, Russian and American, African and Japanese. A tablet from 'the middle wall of partition' in Herod's Temple has recently been discovered. Just as the Bible describes, it bears the threat of execution to all Gentiles who pass that point (Acts 21:26–28). Paul, who knew about it to his cost, writes jubilantly

Now in Christ Jesus, you who once were far away have been brought near through the blood of Christ. For He Himself is our peace, who has made the two one and has destroyed the barrier, the dividing wall of hostility…. His purpose was to create in Himself one new man out of the two…to reconcile both of them to God through the cross…. Through Him do both have access to the Father by one Spirit (Eph 2:13–18).

God's priority at this present time is to create a common-wealth of people that crosses every barrier of country, creed, colour and culture—people *made one* in Jesus. This raises another question. Is it possible to speak of the Jews as exclusively the People of God *without denying the heart of the gospel*?

What is the future for the state of Israel?

Some Christians have a quick answer to that one. The dispensationalism of today's Hal Lindsay and yesterday's *Schofield Reference Bible* says simply that the Kingdom will be given to them…a visible kingdom centred in Jerusalem and ruled by the Messiah, Jesus.

But that has its problems. What exactly is God going to *do* with the Jew? 'Put him back in the Land and one day give him the Kingdom', is the suggested answer. But *what* Kingdom? Jesus' Kingdom, he clearly said, is not of this world (John 18:36). Questioned as to whether he was going to restore the kingdom to Israel he changed the subject and directed the apostles' attention to seeking the power of the Holy Spirit and channelling their energies towards world evangelism (Acts 1:6–8).

An older school of Christian thought, that of the Refor-mation and the Puritans had a slightly different approach. This envisaged a coming powerful work of God when Jews would find the scales fall from their eyes and would turn in considerable numbers to the gospel. Then Jew and Gentile would unite in the great task of evangelism. Some assumed that the Jews would be 'back in their land' before that.

Others felt that was irrelevant; Jews are scattered world-wide, and the gospel is preached worldwide.

The curious fact is that *both* theories have begun to be realised in our lifetime. Jews have returned in their thousands. They have not only a land, but a nation of their own. And now, in increasing numbers, Jews are turning to Jesus. There is a new awareness of him in the land of Israel, a new willingness to look and listen, a new desire to work out his significance. A viable Jewish Church is coming into being in Israel, but even more so in America and other parts of the world. Curiouser and curiouser! We are left with another striking question.

Is it really possible to speak about Israel possessing the Kingdom, when the New Testament describes that kingdom in spiritual terms (as the rule of God, the renewed heart in which God's will is done, and the victory of Jesus at the cross over dark powers?). An hour with a Bible and concordance will rapidly persuade any reader that the Kingdom of God has little to do with real estate, and the People of God have no geographical home, in the Middle East or anywhere else.

This leads to yet another question.

What significance does 'the Land' have today?

Much of the answer to that, we have already explored. The Land is the human stage on which the great drama of redemption has been played out. It roots God's words and Christ's saving acts firmly in real history. The Bible is crammed with images, anecdotes, analogies and promises that are intimately connected with the Land. To the Christian it will always be *His Land*.

But what is its significance *today*? Here we stumble across a staggering fact. Nowhere in the New Testament is the Land made the subject of any divine promise or principle. As a topic, it simply disappears. The great biblical word *inheritance*, which is in the Old Testament almost always meant the physical land, never has that meaning in the New Testament. 'Christ has given us new birth...into an inheritance that can never perish, spoil or fade—kept in heaven for you' (1 Peter 1:4).

As commentators and preachers love to point out, Peter is contrasting what constantly happened to the Jewish earthly inheritance with what cannot happen to the Christian's spiritual inheritance.

Consider the implication of that vivid word-picture employed, by all people, in the letter to the Hebrews: 'You have come to Mount Zion, to the heavenly Jerusalem, the city of the living God...to Jesus the mediator of a new covenant' (Heb 12:22–24).

Coming to Jerusalem means coming to Jesus! I made the point by preaching on that text *in* Jerusalem at the end of one of the Christian 'Tabernacle' gatherings already referred to. Some British Christians thanked me warmly, saying, 'We were beginning to get the impression that the West Bank is the centre of the purposes of God and that the Arabs are the enemy of God!'

Does God's promise to Abraham support the Israeli occupation of Arab lands?

As I write, the words 'Gaza Strip' and 'West Bank' have become common currency in world newscasts. Highly organised disorders are being savagely put down. The situation may calm down again, but meanwhile Israel is sadly tarnishing her international image. How has this come about? In 1967, in a brilliant pre-emptive strike, Israeli Defence Forces routed Arab armies that were mustering (by their own account) to drive the Jews into the sea. In an essentially defensive war, approved by most of the non-Arab world at the time, Israel ensured her survival, created defensible frontiers, and enlarged her territories fourfold.

Their temporary occupation was intended to be a bargaining counter in negotiations for peace, secure borders, the right for Israel to exist, followed by *withdrawal*.

The immediate Arab reply was the famous three negatives of November 1967, 'no peace, no negotiation, no acknowledgement of Israel's right to exist.' After the terrible Yom Kippur War of 1976, Egypt and Israel did in fact negotiate, and Israel handed back huge areas of occupied territory in Sinai. Since then, the situation has festered, worsened by extreme Right attitudes amongst some Jews and recalcitrant hatred from some Arabs.

Two factors have brought that situation to explosion-point. The Palestinian Refugee Camps have remained as running sores. Be clear about this. Israel did not create these camps: they were there when she occupied further land in 1967, because the partition of Palestine in 1948 created refugees from both sides, and Jewish refugees from Arab areas were quickly resettled in Israel. Arab refugees from Israel were kept in wretched camps in Arab Gaza and Jordan, pawns in the power-game whose sufferings would keep the crisis bubbling, and victims of the propoganda and half truths of both sides. They made the pathetic mistake of imagining that the land they had temporarily fled was still theirs. Legally it was, but the cruel facts said otherwise. Israelis simply kept what Arabs abandoned in flight, and tore up the title deeds.

When, sixteen years later, Israel seized Gaza and the West Bank of Jordan, she inherited the camps. The United Nations, pressurised by Arab powers, forbade the dispersion and resettlement of the refugees which Israel was prepared to organise, and took nominal charge of them. To compare Israel with Nazi Germany and to liken the camps to concentration camps, is absurd. To get any analogy, one would have to suppose that the concentration camps in Poland were organised by the Poles, inherited by Germany in a defensive strike against a threatening enemy, and then kept in existence by the insistence of the League of Nations! It is worth recalling that in January 1988, after Israelis had killed forty Palestinians in the West Bank and Gaza, Arabs in Lebanon temporarily lifted their siege of Palestinian camps there, where a thousand had been killed in twelve months.

But there is a second problem: the Israeli Settlements. Large numbers of Jews have settled in the occupied territories, dispossessing the Arabs who were living normally (not in camps), building towns, planting orchards, creating farms, and displaying every intention of remaining there forever. The process has been furthered by the political Right, and by some Jewish religious movements. Jordan West Bank has been renamed Judaea and Samaria, a move laden with emotional and religious significance. The Arabs now see their own lands, no longer bargaining counters in an unwanted negotiation, but seized and settled and claimed as a gift from God.

But is that not so? Many western Christians would support the Israelis' claim. They cite the promises to Abraham 'To your offspring I will give this land' (Genesis 12:7). 'To your descendants I give this land, from the river of Egypt to the great Euphrates' (Gen 15:18).

God's promises are eternal, and can never be rescinded (it is argued). Moreover, when Israel lost the Land through disobedience and idolatory, further promises of return and restoration were made. Isaiah and Zechariah speak lyrically of that restoration.

So, it is reasoned, Israel has a divine mandate to possess the whole Land, and those who resist her are fighting against God. It is a philosophy embraced by the American Religious Right and pressed at the highest levels of American foreign policy. God has promised to bless those who bless Abraham's seed, and curse those who curse them. So a nation will be blessed in so far as it encourages, finances and arms modern Israel. I recall, in similar vein, an English preacher pointing out that every reverse suffered by the British forces in the Falklands campaign followed the day after some failure of a British politician to whole-heartedly support Israel in the UNO.

What should be the Christian's response to this reasoning?

The reasoning proves too much.
The Genesis 15 (and Joshua 1) promises encompass everything from Lebanon to the Nile, from the Mediterranean to the borders of Iran. How can anyone make this a divine mandate to today's Israeli Defence Force? Certainly the most arden Zionist would baulk at it!

The original promise has already been fulfilled.
The Bible repeatedly says this. There was immediate fulfillment under Joshua, and a wider fulfillment during the brief glory of Solomon's reign, when alliances, treaties, trade and religious influence created a kind of theocratic commonwealth covering the very areas listed in the original promises.

'The Lord gave Israel all the land He had sworn to give their forefathers, and they took possession of it and settled there. Not one of all the Lord's good promises to the house of Israel failed; every one was fulfilled' (Josh 21:43 & 45).

Ancient Israel failed to keep her part of the compact.
The repeated warning of the prophets was that personal morality, social justice and religious loyalty were all features of the compact. As we have seen (pp 21–25) the very climate and geology bore witness to this fact. Ultimately military and political weapons were used by God against his covenant-breaking people. The prophet comments sadly: 'They mocked God's messengers, despised his words and scoffed at His prophets until the wrath of the Lord was aroused against His people and there was no remedy' (2 Chron 36:16).

The promises of restoration were also fulfilled long ago.

Within seventy years of exile, survivors were back in the land, rebuilding the temple and restoring the worship. Certainly most, if not all, of the ecstatic pictures painted by Isaiah and Ezekiel found reality in the 6th Century BC. But this time there were no territorial promises, and the difference is striking. Emphasis is much more on character, on worship, on witness and on spiritual renewal. In point of fact the territory physically regained was tiny. But what had God promised this time?

'I will pour water on the thirsty land, and streams on the dry ground; I will pour my Spirit on your offspring, and my blessing on your descendants' (Is 44:3).

'I will gather them from all around and bring them back into their own land.... They will no longer defile themselves with their idols.... They will be my people and I will be their God' (Ezek 37:21–23).

Certainly a physical return is promised. Jews *do* have a right to a homeland in ancient Canaan. It could even be argued that the very scale of some of the Ezekiel promises (chapter 39:28) point to a far greater in-gathering, which we are seeing today. Nevertheless, the whole trend of these Scriptures is towards a *spiritual* restoration. There is no more talk of the Euphrates and the river of Egypt. In sober fact, Israel did return in the 6th Century BC a remarkably different people, purged forever of idolatory, committed to monotheism and witnessing to the truth of God.

The ultimate fulfillment of the promise to Abraham is the coming of Christ and the establishing of his Church.

To that the increasingly 'spiritual' promises were already pointing. The New Testament repeatedly asserts that these promises are now fulfilled in a non-racial non-geographical work of the spirit of God in creating a worldwide fellowship of faith. *The church* is the kingdom of priests promised to Moses (Ex 19:6 & 1 Peter 2:9). *The church* is the restored

Israel promised to Hosea (Hosea 2:23 & Rom 9:23–26). *The church* is the repaired tent of David promised to Amos (Amos 9:11–12 & Acts 15:14–19). *The church* is Isaiah's ruined vineyard restored (Is 5:1–7 & Mat 21:33–44). Most decisively of all, *the church* is the ultimate fulfillment of the promise made to Abraham; that very promise now used to support military occupation of Middle Eastern land.

> Abraham and his offspring received the promise that he would be heir of the world ... the promise comes by faith ... guaranteed to all Abraham's offspring—not only to those who are of the law but also to those who are of the faith of Abraham. He is the father of us all (Rom 4:13–16).

The Scripture foresaw that God would justify the Gentiles by faith, and announced the gospel in advance to Abraham, so those who have faith are blessed along with Abraham, the man of faith.

It is a supreme and bitter irony that in today's Holy Land, two peoples who can equally claim to be physical descendents of Abraham are fighting each other over boundaries, quoting Scriptures that promise a spiritual community of faith without racial or geographical boundaries to Abraham's spiritual descendants!

What then should the Christian attitude be to Israel and the Jewish people?

1. We should recognise the place of the Jew in God's ancient and eternal purposes. Those whom God has loved and chosen can only be treated by us with respect and affection. Anti-semitism is an appalling and grotesque evil spawned (to our shame) in the Christian west. It must be given no houseroom. Notice how Paul describes the Jews (Rom 9:4–5).

2. The Land itself has shared in God's purposes. Christians will rejoice in what God has done in that land, and its place-names will often be on our lips, symbolising as

they do, so much of God's activity and grace. Moreover, we are bound to recognise the intimate relationship between People and Land, underscored in the Bible, and felt profoundly by Jews of all nations, whether or not they reside in Israel-Palestine.

3. Christians will wish to support Israel's right to exist as a secure and sovereign nation. We are bound to see in *alliyah* (the return of Jews to Palestine) something of the providence of a sovereign God. How can it be anything less? But we would be wise not to lock that perception into one particular scheme of prophecy which does not reflect the understanding of the historic churches, and which does little justice to the way the New Testament itself interprets Old Testament promises.

4. Christians should avoid casting the Arabic world into some kind of demonic role. Remember that hatred of Arabs is anti-semitism too! Christianity is already engaged with Islam in a struggle for men's souls, but we should not repeat the mistake of the Crusaders: principalities and powers are engaged, not tanks and missiles.

5. Christians should be praying and working for understanding, justice and peace in the Middle East, particularly bearing up in our prayers the Jewish Christian Church and the Arab Christian Church in that area, and avoiding words and actions that will imperil or compromise them.

Notes

1. Lance Lambert, *Battle for Israel* (Coverdale, 1976) p 111.
2. Lance Lambert, *The Uniqueness of Israel*, (Kingsway Publications, 1980) p 139.

Epilogue

The end of 1985. The taxi was racing down that same winding road, past the ruined village, past the burned-out trucks, past the soaring pines and sunbaked rocks, past the settlements nestled on the slopes and the vineyards lined amongst the red soil. We would be back (we've been back already) but our residence was over. When we returned it would be as visitors once more. Yet we could never be quite the same again. Television newscasts would never look the same. Bible places would never sound the same. Whenever we saw a Jewish *kippah* or Arab *keffya* (headgear) our hearts would lift. We would never read the words 'Our Lord Jesus Christ' without hearing in our hearts the Hebrew version, 'Adonai Yeshua Ha'Meshiah' murmured in Hebrew Christian congregations. We would never read 'Hear oh Israel, the Lord our God is one' without whispering the original 'Shema Israel Adonai' as Jews had echoed that defiant creed of monotheism through the centuries.

In the fourteen months of our residence, we had met, talked to or preached to perhaps 150,000 people. We had related the story of the cross and the empty tomb hundreds of times and found that it never lost its beauty. We had fellowshipped with people who love Christ and express that love in a score of different ways.

About two hundred people had sought us out to ask the way to God. We had seen the church in Jerusalem (harassed, pressed, sometimes confused) praying together, learning together, worshipping together and witnessing together, in a barriers-down situation that bore shining witness to the reconciled community.

There were Christian friends waiting for us at London airport. I carried a diary full of speaking engagements in two continents and several books full of notes.

Soon I would be packing my bags again and queueing at other flight-gates. The preacher had come back from the Promised Land—but the greatest promise travelled with him.

Make disciples of all nations....
And surely I will be with you always.